W9-CSS-340

Tom Crandall, author of *Your Life SPEAKS*, is uniquely equipped to write such a book. His heart burns for a generation to rise up with righteous influence in every realm of society. Through wisdom and insight, he addresses the roadblocks to our destiny with precision and authority. I am so thankful that through his ministry, and now this book, many will find clarity of heart and mind as to our privileged assignment for the day in which we live. I am confident that all who read this book will be challenged and inspired.

BILL JOHNSON

BETHEL CHURCH, REDDING, CA

Our lives were created to showcase the goodness of God, to broadcast His faithfulness, and to expose others to His incredible love. Whether you are aware of it or not, your life is communicating a message to the world. The question is, what is your life saying?

In his new book, *Your Life SPEAKS*, Tom Crandall's wisdom, passion and personal stories will inspire you to discover your life's message. No matter what season of life you're in, this book will challenge you to define your message and clarify your call so that you can deepen your impact on the world.

Now, more than ever, we must learn how to bring hope to the hopeless. The world needs you! Read *Your Life SPEAKS* and discover your God-given voice, understand your influential identity, and embrace your divine destiny. I highly recommend this book!

KRIS VALLOTTON

SENIOR ASSOCIATE LEADER, BETHEL CHURCH, REDDING, CA
CO-FOUNDER OF BETHEL SCHOOL OF SUPERNATURAL MINISTRY
AUTHOR OF SEVERAL BEST-SELLING BOOKS, INCLUDING
THE SUPERNATURAL WAYS OF ROYALTY AND *SPIRIT WARS*

My friend, Tom is an amazing man of God and he lives what he says. Your Life Speaks is a must read for those who want to fulfill their calling. This book will inspire and challenge you to change your world by living the life God has called you to.

JOHN BEVERE

AUTHOR/MINISTER
MESSENGER INTERNATIONAL

So many people have a disconnect between feeling empowered in their faith and really living it out through their identity. How do you wrap your personal faith around the message of God in your life and become the empowered person He meant you to be?

Tom Crandall gives you the tools you need to let your life have a voice. I am grateful that this book was written for you! It is a practical guide, full of the interest that Tom brings to the table through his unique teaching and writing ability. We need people who know how to let their life speak. This book will engage you in a deeper way than ever to help you become one of them!

SHAWN BOLZ

AUTHOR OF *TRANSLATING GOD, GOD SECRETS*, AND *GROWING UP WITH GOD*
TV PERSONALITY AND MINISTER
WWW.BOLZMINISTRIES.COM

Tom Crandall is one of my favorite communicators. His unique ability to influence comes from a perfect mix of passion and practicality anyone can digest. *Your Life SPEAKS* is full of inspiration, but also gives the reader a roadmap for personal growth and transformation. I hope everyone reads this book!

HAVILAH CUNNINGTON

CO-FOUNDER OF TRUTH TO TABLE
AUTHOR OF *STRONGER THAN THE STRUGGLE*

Tom is qualified to write *Your Life SPEAKS* because his life speaks. I have the privilege of being his friend. He lives this message. I know this book will bring great encouragement to your life, and great insight into who Jesus truly is. This book teaches us that Jesus is who He says He is, and He can do what He said He could do. My hope isn't that you only read this book, but you truly receive this message. Let the change begin!

CHRIS DURSO

AUTHOR OF *THE HEIST: HOW GRACE ROBS US OF OUR SHAME*

Your Life SPEAKS comes from a man who has a deep passion for Jesus and to see young people step into their true identity in Christ. What you're about to read is a book that will challenge and inspire you to take a greater ownership of your life and help you realize your life is saying something. The question is, do you know what people are hearing from your life? I challenge you to let this book change you and compel you to impact the world around you.

ERIC JOHNSON

AUTHOR & SPEAKER
BETHEL REDDING

We love Tom Crandall! We are so excited for him to release a book from his heart. He is such a genuine, amazing man. He burns for the heart of God and really loves people.

BRIAN AND JENN JOHNSON

FOUNDERS, BETHEL MUSIC

I am excited to endorse Tom's book - not because I have read every word, but because I know the man. He's a man passionate about everything he does and everyone he comes into contact with. I don't know anyone better at encouraging youth to find out who they are and why they are alive. He does family well, does ministry well, lives for the gospel to be preached and received and just does life well.

Since leaving Redding, California I can honestly say that sitting next to Tom on the front row at Bethel Church is one of the things I miss the most. His constant encouragement is contagious. I am certain that as you read this book you will get to know this man. He will infect your life with a passion for Jesus and being about the Father's business.

PAUL MANWARING

SENIOR TEAM, BETHEL REDDING

As a teenager at Young Saints, I have experienced firsthand Tom's burning passion to see every young person fully alive and aware of the power of Christ inside of them! *Your Life SPEAKS* isn't just another self-help book. The honest truths and raw examples in this book challenged me to examine the message my life is speaking, and to decide if that message is worth replicating. If you are up for the same challenge, this book is for you! The tools laid out within the chapters, the Holy Spirit's encouragement, and a desire to change the world around you will jump-start your life into speaking a message full of passion and power!

HOSANNA KUMMER

SENIOR AT FOOTHILL HIGH SCHOOL, REDDING, CA

YOUR
LIFE
SPEAKS

FINDING YOUR VOICE OF
INFLUENCE FOR YOUR GENERATION

TOM CRANDALL

Cover Design by Samantha Rouse
Interior Design by Scottie A.B.

ISBN: 978-1-947165-30-4

Printed in the United States.

TABLE OF CONTENTS

ACKNOWLEDGMENTS

To the fathers in my life at Bethel Church: Bill Johnson, Kris Vallotton, Danny Silk, Paul Manwaring, and Steve Backlund. Thank you for fighting for the faith we get to walk in. You have changed my life, believed in me, and fought for me. I will be forever grateful.

To my beautiful wife, best friend, and love, Leslie Crandall. Your life speaks so loudly that everyone wants to hear what you have to say. Thank you for believing in me and helping me become the man God sees. I love you forever.

To my kids, Joel and Adelyn. You are the joy of my life and my greatest treasure on earth. I am so proud of you both!

To the Young Saints staff and youth leaders. You are the dream team! Thank you for believing God with me and working so hard to see God touch a generation! It is such an honor to run with you.

To Young Saints. You guys are radical lovers of Jesus! It's time to *let your lives speak* so loudly that Redding comes to your light—that none in our city perish, but find hope because you were born.

Trey Ellis, thank you for inspiring me to write. Your skills and belief were a big help in completing the work.

To you, the reader. Thank you for picking up this book. My prayer is that no matter your background, color, or nation, you will find yourself encountering God on each page. May you be transformed until your life speaks of Jesus and how He sees you, till your friends, social media page, school, and city comes to know what you are carrying.

FOREWORD

BY BANNING LIEBSCHER

Many years ago, Shadrach, Meshach, and Abednego found themselves in a critical moment—a moment to decide whether they would let their lives speak, or shut up and obey the intimidating voice of their culture. These three young revivalists had experienced the call of God on their lives at an early age, and had set themselves apart for Him while living in the godless nation of Babylon. But the day came in which King Nebuchadnezzar called the nation to gather and bow down to an image he had set up—or be executed. Under threat of death, Babylonians, Chaldeans, and even Israelites all prostrated themselves to the image.

Shadrach, Meshach, and Abednego refused to bow down.

When Nebuchadnezzar heard about their stand, he summoned them in anger and told them if they didn't bow, he would throw them into the fire to die. But threats and intimidation do not easily sway those who know who they are. Shadrach, Meshach, and Abednego refused to silence their voice in self-preservation. They stood their ground, and let themselves be thrown into the furnace.

Then God Himself showed up. His three guys came out of the fire without even smelling like smoke! And what happened next? *An entire nation turned to God.*

My entire ministry life, I have given myself to seeing a generation awakened. It has been my burning passion to see youth and young adults find their identity completely in Christ and to stand securely, even when those around them are bowing to the influence of the surrounding culture.

I have witnessed firsthand that the same spirit of intimidation is alive and well today, and it is aggressively trying to get a generation to sit down and shut up. As I once heard a speaker say, the enemy is not scared of Christians; he is scared of certain Christians—those who are securely planted in their identity in Christ and have found their voice. But despite hell's efforts, God is awakening a generation through His love and power, teaching them their identity, and causing their voices to be heard. The awakening that is happening in this generation will awaken our nation and bring about the greatest harvest in all of history.

Your Life SPEAKS is not just a book to read, but a call to take hold of your identity in Christ and your place in this generation. It is critical in this hour that you not only realize that your life speaks, but also that you take responsibility for your life. God has placed on you a mandate to change the world. That is not hyperbole to excite you; it is the truth found throughout Scripture. You were born to make a difference. You were created to do the impossible. You were called to be part of the greatest revival the world has ever seen. May you hear His voice calling you in the testimonies and teaching of this book, and let His voice speak through your life with boldness. As you do, He will show up and back you up—just as He did for Meshach, Shadrach, and Abednego.

BANNING LIEBSCHER,

FOUNDER AND PASTOR OF JESUS CULTURE

INTRODUCTION

In one word, *Your Life SPEAKS* is about *influence.*

The influence we allow in our lives, the choices we make, the encounters that mark us, and what we give ourselves to—these are what our lives SPEAK.

Do you know what your life SPEAKS?

We only have one shot at life. There is no re-do.

We live in a nation struggling with racial tension and political division, in which the pressure to hide your faith is intensifying. The world is starving to hear from God, and God has placed His presence on us so our lives can SPEAK of power and love for them to hear. I wrote this book with you in mind, because you and I are God's Plan A for this broken world. He has no Plan B.

The pressure to be like everyone else has been supercharged by social media and the Internet, and this pressure is robbing a generation of their ability to SPEAK from who they really are. I believe this generation is hungry for a fresh touch from God, and they are looking for real answers. I've done my best to write an unfiltered, raw book with real stories of kids and adults who let their lives SPEAK solutions of hope in today's world.

It's time to get your hopes up!

No matter what your life SPEAKS today, you can receive an upgrade for tomorrow. I believe you are holding this book in your hand because you are carrying hope for a brighter tomorrow. If you're not satisfied with letting your life SPEAK of the status quo, but are ready to do whatever it takes to see revival touch those around you, then let's go on this journey together.

If there has ever been a time that we need to rise up and let our lives SPEAK hope and love, it's now.

Will you let your life SPEAK?

TOM CRANDALL
YOUTH PASTOR
YOUNG SAINTS, REDDING, CA

"

HE IS NO FOOL WHO GIVES WHAT HE CANNOT KEEP TO GAIN THAT WHICH HE CANNOT LOSE.

"

JIM ELLIOT

MISSIONARY TO ECUADOR, MARTYR

CHAPTER [1]

WHAT DOES YOUR LIFE SPEAK?

I was eighteen, and I was at a Halloween party wearing the worst costume *ever*. Sitting in my backyard with a beer in my hand, surrounded by drunk "friends," I became overwhelmed with a feeling of emptiness. It didn't make sense to me. I was supposed to be "having fun" like everyone else seemed to be. I thought I had everything I wanted in life. I was a successful athlete at school, popular among my friends, and dating constantly. Still, I could not shake the feeling of worthlessness. It felt like my life didn't matter. My success and happiness felt meaningless. There had to be more to life than just doing whatever felt good and looked good.

I took another sip of my beer, looked up towards the sky, and whispered these words to myself: "What am I *doing*?"

In that moment, something happened in my heart. Even though my decision to change something (anything!) seemed small and insignificant, it started a series of events that would change the course of my entire life.

[THE FIFTY-YARD JOURNEY]

After that night, I did the only thing I could think of to try to find something that would give me purpose. I started going to church and reading my Bible.

At first, I tried inviting my friends to come to church with me, but they just laughed and mocked me for "doing the Jesus thing." That hurt. For much of my life, I had done whatever I thought other people would like and accept. But what had that done for me? Where did that ever take me? I was starting to realize that living for the approval and acceptance of other people was a path that led to the very lifestyle of hopelessness that I was trying to come out of. So, though I continued to party with my friends on the weekends, I also continued to go to church every weekend without them. Over the next six months, my hunger for God grew steadily.

Then one Sunday night, the speaker at church closed his talk with an invitation: "If you want more of God, then come up front."

I looked at my dad and said, "I'm going to go down there."

After making what seemed like a fifty-mile journey from the back, I sat down in the front of the church and prayed a simple prayer: "God, I'm here."

I wasn't ready for what happened next. I felt the presence of God overshadow and envelop me. I could feel His all-knowing eyes look through my soul as I heard these words: *"I'm cleansing you."* His liquid love pierced through every part of me as His all-powerful arms wrapped around me, making me feel safe, forgiven, and accepted. I was crying so hard that I had snot hanging from my face to the floor as my hot tears flowed. I had just met everything I had been looking for—a God outside of time with unending love and forgiveness, who had become more real to me than the carpet I was sitting on. I also knew that though I had been pursuing God for a short time, He had been pursuing me my whole life.

I got up from the ground with a heart that wanted to please God. Every other opinion that controlled my life died that day. I knew I was alive for one thing—to please the Lord of my life. My mind shifted from living for this life, to living to please the eternal God, who is completely good. *And because God's opinion of my life now mattered the most, He began to shape the message my life would begin to SPEAK.*

[THE DEATH OF SELFIE]

After this encounter with God, I discovered that in surrendering to Him as Lord and putting my trust in Him, some amazing things had happened to me. The old Tom hadn't just gotten an upgrade—he had *died* with Christ on the cross! He wasn't just forgiven—he had come to life again!

Jesus referred to this experience of radical transformation when He said, "No one can see the kingdom of God unless they are *born again*."[1] To be born again means to have an experience where your old life dies and you get a new life. It's not something you can earn or religiously try to obtain. The only way you can be born again is when Jesus touches your life, and you turn away from your old life and turn towards Him to receive the new life He has for you.

Jesus didn't just move into the guesthouse of my life. He came in to every room of my life and became the Lord of all. His power conquered my heart with love and gave me a new operating system that empowered me to live like Him on the earth. My desires changed, my perspective changed, and my heart became soft and motivated by love. The dry, crusty attitude that came from a life of sin and selfishness was broken, and the innocent boy I once knew in my childhood was alive again. I began to live a new life.

---

[1] John 3:3 NIV, my emphasis

What about you? Have you been born again? I'm not asking if you were raised in church. Has Jesus become the Lord of your life?

Yes, turning in your old life for the new one Jesus wants to give you will cost you your old life. We all have to count the cost. You may not yet be at the point where you're ready to let go of what you have. Or, you may be where I was that night at the Halloween party. At that point, I already knew, deep down, that keeping my old life was going to cost me far more in the end than it cost to give it up.

Though I had been raised in a Christian home and had encountered God as a child, what I chose in junior high and high school caused the story of my life to go astray from the manuscript of joy and peace. It's been said before: "Once you make your choices, your choices make you." Our choices in life determine what our lives *speak*. I had chosen to ignore the Holy Spirit and go against God's Word. I had allowed my life to become driven by the waves of what other people thought and the winds of what would make me cool. I had allowed fear and peer pressure to rob me of letting my life speak. My life spoke of one person: me. Gross!

For some, this may seem like an ideal way of living—to selfishly indulge in the drama of life, doing whatever it takes to get the most followers on Instagram, to have the best style, and to feel loved by everyone. After all, that's the playbook the world is throwing at us for freedom and happiness. If it feels good, do it. If it's cool, who cares—you are free to do whatever you want. Smoke it if you've got it, have sex with whoever whenever, watch whatever, listen to whatever—it's not going to hurt anyone and no one cares.

Lies! The wages of sin is death.[2] If you fill your gas tank with saltwater, you're going to break down.

___

[2] Romans 6:23

I wouldn't want anyone to repeat some of the costly choices I made as a teenager. Therefore I am making myself vulnerable so others can learn and choose differently. The consequences of my choices were painful. By the night of that Halloween party, I had reached the point where I felt tired, like a broken-down car in the middle of the desert. Ignoring the "check engine" light on the dashboard of my heart had left me stalled out on the freeway of depression in a desert of loneliness and confusion. My life of athletics and my free-spirited personality were a cover for shame, regret, and a longing for a way out. It looked like I had tons of friends, but I was really alone and afraid. My eighteen-year-old heart was crying out for something different than what I had tasted so far in my teen years. I had no language to describe the storm of pain, confusion, and fear inside me, but I knew my choice to ignore heaven's signals wasn't helping me.

I had blown past many stop signs on my drive into self-absorption. It's intriguing that God will give us warnings, but doesn't take away our freedom to choose while He waits patiently for our attention. For example, one stop sign God used to protect me was my dad, who once told me when I was in seventh grade, "I don't want you hanging out with those friends. They are a bad influence." I wish I could say I listened to my dad, but I didn't. At the time, I viewed my friends, who were mocking me for going to church, as more of an annoyance that made my choice a little bit harder to choose. When I rededicated my life at eighteen, I realized that God had used my friends in two ways—first, to show me that my choice to follow Him would cost me something, and then to show me that choosing to go along with the crowd would cost me even more in the end.

We are all looking for fulfillment. Whatever we pursue to fulfill our lives is what our lives will SPEAK. The world tells us to take in order to get, consume in order to live, and embrace everything we feel to really have a life. We chase illusions of fulfillment on social media. We've all seen the guy or girl who looks like they have it all, compare the inside of our world to the outside of theirs, and feel like we never measure up. Before we know it, we are running a fear-driven rat race in the desire to be the coolest, have the most stuff, or be top dog. But does that give you the life you really want? It didn't for me! And I don't see it offering true fulfillment for anyone else. All it does is turn us into self-absorbed people who live to please one person—ourselves. And our lives SPEAK selfishly.

What about you? As long as you have breath in your lungs, you can change what your life is speaking with a choice. For me, it all started with the smallest prayer: "God, I need You. If You can hear me, help."

He is faithful. Like a flashlight in a forest, you may not be able to see far ahead, but He will always show you the next step towards a fulfilling life.

[LOVE IS WORTH THE PRICE]

If you are having a hard time surrendering your life to God, then you probably haven't seen the depth of His love for you yet. The moment you truly taste His love for you, as I did, you will know that He is worth any price.

In 1997, I left home to attend a school of ministry in Pensacola, Florida. It was there that I met Leslie Lahr—the most beautiful girl I had ever seen. She had long brown hair, a contagious smile, a spunky personality, and a love for God that spoke louder than words.

I led street evangelism teams on Friday nights, and when she joined my team I was elated! We began to spend time together in groups of friends. The more I got to know her, the more I liked her and could see myself with her. By the second semester of ministry school, this girl had captured my heart.

However, Leslie had been in a previous relationship that ended painfully, and she was still working through that as we developed a friendship. By the time early spring had come, we had both expressed feelings for each other, but she wasn't ready to commit her heart to me yet because she was still healing from the pain of the past. When she communicated this to me, my response was that I would wait as long as she needed. This beautiful person was worth any price to me.

Leslie and I continued to develop a friendship, and I gave her the space she needed to heal. When school started up again in the fall, we hung out in friend groups, continued to do street evangelism, and pursued God together. Soon, she let me know that her heart had healed and she was ready to move forward with our relationship.

During winter break, I flew to Pennsylvania to meet her family. Her parents live on a farm, so I got to know her dad by running a chainsaw in the woods, cutting firewood to heat the house, and doing other work together. After mustering up enough courage while standing by the outdoor grill, I asked him for permission to pursue his daughter with the intention of marriage. He said yes!

Then, on January 7, 1999, I proposed to Leslie, and she said yes! We finished out our final semester of ministry school in Pensacola as an engaged couple. That summer, she moved back to Pennsylvania and I to Utah. We wrote letters to each other of our love and affection and planned our wedding by phone.

The first book I ever wrote was to my soon-to-be wife. Before we got engaged, I bought a journal and wrote my first entry on April 24, 1998. For over a year, I wrote to Leslie about our relationship without her knowing. I wrote about the events that shaped our lives in the revival we were part of in Pensacola, and our growing love for each other. It was a fun process, though it was also a lot of work, and required a lot of thought and time. However, it was worth every second! I wrote my final entry on September 11, 1999—the day Leslie became my wife—and gave her the journal on our wedding night. Today, as I write this book, we are celebrating eighteen years of marriage. She is my best friend and the greatest gift God has ever entrusted to me. I love her more than life.

There was no price I wouldn't pay to love this beautiful girl who had captivated my heart. I lost myself by laying down all other options, because I saw only one that mattered.

This is what it is like with God! When we see His beauty and goodness, we are invited into a divine romance of the heart that will not leave us disappointed. Happiness and fulfilment aren't found in getting more, but in giving away what we have. Many of us do things in the name of love, when really it just benefits ourselves. This is not love. Love benefits others at the expense of self, not the other way around. God is love, and when we allow His love to transform us, our lives become a response to His love. We give ourselves to Him as He gave—and gives—Himself to us.

Nothing this world offers compares to His great love. Years ago, I visited Niagara Falls. It was unbelievable to watch an immeasurable amount of water fall over a cliff into a swelling cloud of mist as it joined the river below. It made an impression on my heart that I could never get on a screen. Nothing manmade could provoke such wonder and awe. Yet I feel even greater wonder and awe when I consider how Creator God wrapped Himself in human flesh and died on the cross in the place of fallen humanity. On that day, blood and water flowed from His body, touching earth and creating a way for all people to receive redemption and forgiveness. The cross is the signpost of His love and the price tag of our value. It's where we find out what our lives are worth—the cost of God's perfect Son. He paid the ultimate price so we could be healed and have unbroken friendship with Him regardless of our history. Jesus didn't go to the cross so He could tolerate us, but to be with us now. Jesus loves us! How could I respond to the beauty of such unconditional love except by giving Him everything?

Years ago, my wife had the opportunity to smuggle Bibles into China and meet with some pastors there—some of whom had spent over twenty years in prison because of their faith in Christ. These brave men said they would do it all over again because they loved Jesus and He was worth it to them. When you taste His love for you, you know there is no price too high to pay to love Him in return. As a missionary named Jim Elliot, who died giving his life away for Jesus, said, "He is no fool who gives up what he cannot keep in order to gain what he cannot lose."

Jesus said:

"If anyone desires to come after Me, let him deny himself, and take up his cross daily, and follow Me. For whoever desires to save his life will lose it, but whoever loses his life for My sake will save it. For what profit is it to a man if he gains the whole world, and is himself destroyed or lost?"[3]

What about you? How is the Holy Spirit drawing you closer to Jesus today? Are you still hanging on to what everyone else says about you and allowing your life to speak a message that doesn't reflect who you really are? Are you trying to save your life by being too cool to share what God has done in you out of fear of being rejected? If you've already lost your life, what can they reject?

[JESUS' MISSION]

For three and a half years, the Son of God walked the earth and revealed to humanity what God looks like. His life only spoke of what He saw the Father doing. He healed blind eyes, raised the dead, and loved the ones religion sought to condemn. Though blameless, He took on the consequences of our sinful choices and died in our place so we could live. As a result, He became the most influential human in the history of the world.

Jesus also wasn't afraid to offend people to help them get free from themselves. Jesus told one man—the "rich young ruler"—that he lacked one thing to find eternal life. Jesus told him he needed to sell all he had, give the proceeds to the poor, pick up his cross, and follow Him. The man was sad and walked away because he wasn't willing to do it at that time. Jesus' point wasn't just telling the man to sell it all—it was to give him the opportunity to see the value of what he had compared to the priceless treasure he would get in following Jesus. He looked at the Author of riches, and chose an inferior reward.

Jesus didn't tell everyone to sell all they had. He always speaks to each person in a way that addresses where they are and what they need to do to step into relationship with Him. He said to Peter and Andrew, "Follow Me, and I will make you fishers of men."[4] He said to Matthew, "Follow me."[5] Another man, whom Jesus set free from a couple thou-

[4] Matthew 4:18
[5] Mark 2:14

sand demons, wanted to follow the Lord, but Jesus sent him home to his friends to announce what He had done for him.[6] Others He didn't say anything to—He just healed them and that was it.

What *is* required from you in a relationship with Jesus is that you let go of whatever would replace your trust and affection for Jesus and follow Him. Jesus isn't afraid of you having money. He just doesn't want your money to have you. He isn't scared of you being popular. He just wants to make sure you use your popularity to serve others, not yourself. When money and popularity are your source of happiness, you're dependent on outward circumstances for everything—your identity, security, happiness, and hope. This is why Jesus challenged these things individually. The Holy Spirit is faithful to deal with those things in our hearts that hinder love and purpose. Our source of life is, and must be, Him. When we depend on Him for our identity, security, happiness, and hope, then money and popularity can become tools to let our lives speak of His love and power.

When you lose your life, God gives your life back to you, and no one can take away your relationship with Jesus. If you want fulfilment, it's time to lose your life for Jesus. Then you will find it!

[WILL YOUR LIFE SPEAK HOPE?]

Jesus' ultimate goal was not just to die for our sins. He came to find a people through whom He could live His life. Yes, He came to save us from sin, death, and hell, but many stop right there and just wait to go to heaven. The point of salvation isn't to go to heaven when we die. It's to get heaven *in us* so we can take it to the rest of the planet.

---

[6] Mark 5:19

If you're currently on a school campus, whether it's junior high, senior high, or college, you're living in the biggest mission field in America. While many people are removing their light, influence, and voices from the world, God wants to send us to bring hope and love to those who need it. The world needs what you are carrying! The church shouldn't be a bunker we hide in, but a training ground to learn how to bring heaven to earth and let our lives SPEAK.

The world is starving for hope—for something real, loving, and tangible that moves them at their core. Hope isn't wishful thinking; it is the confident expectation that good is coming—that no matter how it feels right now, something better is coming. It's why people dropped everything to follow Jesus. He offered them real hope.

I will never forget when a fourteen-year-old girl approached me following a message I had given and asked, "Is it really true? Can I be forgiven and restored from losing my virginity?"

"Yes!" I said. I released restoration and hope to her.

In Australia, one teenage girl thanked me following a youth conference I spoke at. She explained that she had been abused by her father and was really bitter and hurt. But after encountering God, she realized He was a good Father. Hope for her life and future was restored to her.

In Siberia, Russia, I was prophesying over a man and said, "I just see hope over you."

He looked at me in surprise, and said, "My wife's name is Hope." He got rocked by the love of God and felt so known in that moment.

At Bethel, we say, "The person with the most hope has the most influence." Some of the most influential people in my life have given me the most hope. The choices they made inspired me and gave me hope for my future. And they also showed me the power we release into people's lives when we offer them true hope.

You are called to be a hope-bringer. It's in your DNA. Hope isn't something you have to strive for; it's something you receive as a follower of Jesus. He is the hope of the nations. Carrying hope simply means bringing Jesus into every situation you face.

One of the hope-bringers in this generation is a young man named Caleb, who attended my youth group in Salt Lake City, Utah before I moved to Redding to lead Young Saints at Bethel. Caleb was an ordinary young man who locked himself in his room to pray and seek the Lord, and encountered God. After that encounter, he began devouring books by revivalists like Smith Wigglesworth and others, and grew rapidly in his faith.

Meanwhile, Caleb got a job as a lifeguard at a local aquatic center. After finishing his training, he was asked to be hired on early because of his audit results. He was nervous to accept, but he felt God say, "Do it. I have something for you."

He thought, *Heck, Lord, is someone going to die?* But he took the job.

Caleb's first day was May 2, 2011. That day was completely uneventful until his last rotation of the day. As he was about to step off his stand, he heard a man say, "Help him!"

Caleb looked to his left and saw a man trying to pull his friend, who appeared to be completely limp, out of the pool. Caleb and the other lifeguards immediately understood that this was a real emergency. Their team jumped into action. After taking the man's pulse and discovering that there was none, they began CPR. Two minutes later, they connected him to an AED defibrillator to detect whether he was getting a pulse again. Though it's generally advised not to administer electric shock when there's no pulse, the team made the call to give the man two shocks, but to no avail. Seven minutes passed, and the man still had no pulse.

Caleb knew that after four minutes without oxygen to the brain and spine, a person is considered biologically dead. As he stood at the man's head observing him, it suddenly struck him that he was looking down at a dead man. At that moment, something clicked inside Caleb. He knew he must pray for the man. He stretched out his hand and prayed a very simple prayer aloud: "Jesus, have Your way."

Immediately, the man sat up, eyes wide open. He began to cough up blood and foam. After a few moments, he was able to breathe normally, and lay back down to rest.

A week later, Caleb met with this man. His name was Kevin, and he was twenty-one years old. Caleb knew he was looking at a miracle. Statistically, Kevin had 0.001 percent chance of surviving from drowning. After beating those odds, there was a 99.99 percent chance that he would be a total vegetable. Those are unexaggerated facts. Kevin had no damage to his brain or spinal cord. Not only that, the doctor had watched his lungs heal from 60 percent effective (because of the water damage) and become 100-percent, brand-new lungs. They knew Kevin had new lungs because he had been a smoker before the incident. Lungs don't heal like that. Everyone involved admitted it was a healing. Kevin even acknowledged that it was Jesus who raised and healed him, and that he was grateful!

Caleb told me that when he prayed for Kevin, he didn't feel like he had any faith. He simply prayed out of instinct. He didn't have time to question where his faith level was. But Jesus had His way.

From that day on, everyone who worked with Caleb began asking him questions about his faith. Why? Because his life spoke of power that gave a man's life back. He was able to point them to Jesus. Most of the employees he worked with were not Christians, and wouldn't normally have listened to anything he had to say. Working as a lifeguard was never the same.

Caleb lost his life to really let it speak—and hope is what everyone heard. In the same way, people are looking for *your life* to give them hope, so their dead dreams can come to life. For some people, we are the only Bible they have had the opportunity to read.

What about you? It's your turn!

"

WHATEVER WE ALLOW TO

INFLUENCE

US WILL DETERMINE THE
MESSAGE OUR LIFE SPEAKS.

"

TOM CRANDALL
#YOURLIFESPEAKS

CHAPTER [2]

THE POWER OF INFLUENCE

Mari was sixteen when I became her youth pastor. She was a typical American teenager who loved life, friends, and fun. Over time, I got to know Mari and noticed the influence some of her friends were having on her. If she didn't do what they wanted when they wanted it, they would shame her and make her feel bad till she bowed to their tyrannical demands.

Leslie and I had many conversations with Mari, and eventually told her that based on our observations, it was likely that she had formed and unhealthy *soul tie* with her friends.

If you've ever had a close friend you constantly thought about and couldn't live without, then you've probably had a *soul tie.* A soul tie is an agreement between you and another person that joins you together in spirit and soul, giving the other person high levels of influence in your life. When your relationship is sexual, you become joined with the other person in spirit, soul, and body, making it the most binding type of soul tie.

A soul tie is an opportunity for two people to become "one" with each other. Your level of intimacy determines the power of the soul tie and the level of influence you have with each other. This is positive when it's healthy, and destructive when it's not. The bond between a parent and child is a powerful soul tie, in which both receive and give love and strength. Marriage is a healthy and powerful soul tie where two become one. However, anything sexual outside of a commitment of marriage becomes destructive, because it's giving the highest level of influence in your life to another without the commitment to protect you. (This is why porn is so destructive—you are having sexual encounters with images of people with whom you have no connection. This creates soul ties with a demonic, self-destructive spirit that will always leave you empty and craving more. It robs you of both present joy and future fulfillment.) Time and time again, I've watched kids crash or soar in life based upon the soul ties they formed with friends and in dating relationships.

After we described the nature and effects of soul ties to Mari, she recognized that she needed to deal with her fear of her friends and their opinions. We then explained to her that soul ties can be broken by repenting for giving them a place of influence and speaking to the soul tie to be broken in the name of Jesus. Mari decided to do just that. She renounced her soul ties with her friends, pulled away from their influence, and began to replace their influence with God and healthy friends. She started to spend time in the secret place with Jesus and hang out with other believers who spoke life to her. Soon, Mari's life began to change dramatically and SPEAK a totally different message. Instead of speaking of fear and manipulation, her life began to speak of love.

Soul ties are fueled by either fear or love. Fear controls, but love liberates. Mari's soul tie with her old friends was fueled by fear, and her life demonstrated patterns of manipulation, intimidation, and control. Mari was afraid of what her friends thought about her, and it kept her from thinking for herself. Her new relationships with God and other believers, on the other hand, were fueled by love, and as a result, she was set free to choose what her life would SPEAK. Her life went from controlled to confident, lost to loving, and from exasperated to an example for others to follow. Her life began to SPEAK so much that when she spoke, everyone wanted to hear what she had to say.

Just this year, we decided to hire Mari as our youth worship leader. When she gave notice at the dentist's office where she had been working that she was leaving to take the job with us, her boss told her, "Mari you should be really proud about the impact you have had at this practice. You have not only impacted me, but you also have impacted every single person who is part of this office staff! You have impacted them not just by what you have said, but by the way you live your life." Mari's life speaks wherever she goes—just because she made the simple, yet powerful choice to break her soul ties with toxic friendships and follow Jesus at sixteen years old.

[KILLING THE INFLUENCE OF COMPARISON]

Whoever you fear controls your life. If you fear a tyrant, you'll never think outside the boundaries they set for you. Fear a bully, and you'll obey him. Fear the devil, and you give him power over your life.

Along with unhealthy soul ties, one of the most common ways we open the door to the influence of fear is through comparison. Have you ever been on social media scrolling through images of everyone else's life, and started to feel like garbage when you looked at your own? That's the spirit of comparison, which is really the spirit of fear with a mask on. Comparison is not always easy to recognize, but it always makes us feel like we don't measure up. We compare the inside of our world to the outside of everyone else's, and lose every time. Comparison is a vicious master that never allows its victims to think for themselves. Like a bully stealing your lunch money, it seeks to intimidate you into giving up your value and identity by making you feel like his muscles are always bigger. You feel like you're not enough, so you don't even try to stand up to him and just hand over what is rightfully yours.

When we react to the spirit of comparison by attempting to post things on social media that make us look cool enough, we usually don't look cool—but we do look desperate. We wear ourselves out and sacrifice the joy of who God has created us to be!

I've heard stories of girls who enter the modeling industry and give up their natural beauty, starving themselves in order to compare to what the industry thinks beautiful looks like. Rather than owning and celebrating their originality, they conform to the status quo, which is deeply unhealthy. Their lives are robbed from the inside out, and then thrown out when the system is done with them.

Two things help you kill the influence of comparison in your life. First, you need to know and believe who God says you are. If we all really knew who we were, we would never struggle with comparison again. My kids don't struggle too much with trying to be like other kids, because they know how awesome, good-looking, and talented they are. Why? Because they hear it from their parents all the time! And they know Leslie and I aren't just expressing our own opinions; we're speaking the truth of what God says about them. As a result, they are confident in themselves.

You have been created in the image and likeness of God, who has never created junk—only masterpieces! When you allow what God says over you to be the main influence in your life, comparison will become easier to recognize, and you will have the power to resist the lies the enemy is throwing at you.

The second thing that helps us kill comparison is gratitude. When I recognize the spirit of comparison, I have strength to resist it and not partner with it. I back up, turn my phone off, and start thanking God for who I am and how He has blessed me. I know it doesn't sound flashy, but it's true, and it works. Being thankful is an act of faith that aligns our thoughts with His and shuts down fear that we aren't enough or that we are missing out in life.

[THE INFLUENCE OF THE KINGDOM]

The truth is that fear and love are influences rooted in the spirit realm. Fear is rooted in the kingdom of darkness, and love is rooted in the kingdom of God.

These spiritual kingdoms are clashing in America right now on race, gender, politics, what makes you cool, the definition of family, the supposed many ways to God, and the list goes on. But throughout time, there is only one kingdom that remains, and that's the one God revealed in the person of Jesus Christ in Scripture—the kingdom of God.

When Jesus started preaching, He said, "Repent, for the kingdom of heaven [or kingdom of God] is near."[1] *Repent* simply means to change the way you think. *Kingdom* means the sphere or realm where the king reigns. Kings are powerful, and when they show up, everything under their influence begins to take shape as they see fit. The kingdom of God (or kingdom of heaven) is the spiritual realm where King Jesus reigns. Jesus came to demonstrate to an orphan planet what the ultimate good Father is like. God looks like Jesus, because Jesus is God. Jesus healed all who came to Him, He covered and forgave sinners that the religious sought to con-

---

[1] Matthew 4:17, Mark 1:14

demn, and laid down His own life for everyone, paying the ultimate price for our freedom. What king has done that? As Bill Johnson says, "Everyone wants a king like Jesus!" Jesus didn't, and doesn't, come with military might forcing people to follow Him, but with love, grace, and truth, inviting the world into relationship with Him through the Holy Spirit and the Word of God.

Jesus' mission was for the influence of this kingdom of love to come into our lives and transform us, then flow through us to the world. Jesus told His disciples, "I grant to you a kingdom, just as my Father granted to me."[2] He told us to "seek the kingdom of God" confidently, knowing that "it is [our] Father's good pleasure to give [us] the kingdom."[3] He also explained that we receive this kingdom when we receive the Holy Spirit.[4]

Before Jesus came, everyone was influenced from the outside in through the controlling power of fear wielded by the kingdom of darkness. But now, the kingdom of love that Jesus brought lives inside our hearts and minds, so we live powerfully from the inside out. One of the most incredible illustrations of this inside-out kingdom is the way Jesus treated lepers. Before Jesus came, if you touched a leper, you got leprosy. But when Jesus touched lepers, they got healed. That is the healing, restoring power of God's love and life that flows through us when we receive Jesus. This is *huge*! There is a river of life, of heaven's reality, flowing from the throne of God, through our hearts, and to the world around us.

We align ourselves to be influenced by the kingdom of God by surrendering our lives to King Jesus and His Word. When we turn away from trusting our own ways and trust

---

[2] Luke 22:29 NET

[3] Luke 12:31-32 NKJV

[4] Acts 1:5 NLT

Him, we will begin to do what He asks of us, and our lives will begin to SPEAK of the hope this world needs!

Do you see any areas in your life that you need to surrender to Jesus? He is waiting to empower you as you surrender to Him. How is the Holy Spirit encouraging you to change today?

[INFLUENCED BY ETERNITY]

All of humanity has one thing in common. We are all going to die one day and stand before God to give an account for our lives. Dang! It's not a popular subject, but it's real!

The Bible says that all of humanity will either stand before the great, white throne of judgment or the judgment seat of Christ. The great white throne will be for those who rejected God's gift of His Son Jesus, and He will give them what they wanted in this life—a life apart from Him.[5] And the judgment seat of Christ is for believers, where they will be rewarded for the life of faith they lived and welcomed into eternity with Him.[6]

The word *judgment seat* isn't as scary as we think. It means *a place where a judge decides, or a place where decisions are made*.[7] God is not like an evil stepmother waiting to bring up our failures. Sin was forgiven for all eternity at the cross, so if we've put our faith in Christ to make us right before God, we can know when we stand at the judgment seat of Christ that we've already been forgiven. The merciful and gracious Judge, Father God, will reward us for the life of obedience we lived. If we lived selfishly with our faith, we won't receive the same reward as those who lived faithfully, but we will still enter into the joy of the Lord.

---

[5] Revelation 20:11-13

[6] 2 Corinthians 5:10

[7] *Greek English Lexicon of the New Testament Based on Semantic Domains*, s.v. "bema."

The reality of eternity hit me after my encounter with God. I believe it is perhaps one of the most important revelations this generation needs. Most people are simply living for today, and ignoring the fact that their life will continue beyond this one. Scripture says that "[God] has planted eternity in the human heart."[8] C.S. Lewis referred to our God-planted desire for eternity when he wrote:

> If I find in myself desires which nothing in this world can satisfy, the only logical explanation is that I was made for another world... I must take care, on the one hand, never to despise, or be unthankful for, these earthly blessings, and on the other, never to mistake them for the something else of which they are only a kind of copy, or echo, or mirage. I must keep alive in myself the desire for my true country, which I shall not find till after death... I must make it the main object of my life to press on to that other country and to help others to do the same.[9]

If we choose to see life through the lens of eternity, a lot of stuff that doesn't matter will simply fall away from our lives. Ask yourself: "How are the things I am presently living for going to affect me five minutes after I step into eternity?"

Eternity matters when thinking about what your life SPEAKS. If you are living with an eternal mindset, it won't matter to you as much when people criticize you, because their opinion has an expiration date. When you live for eternity, the expiration date for negative criticism is always *now*.

---

[8] Ecclesiastes 3:11 NLT
[9] C.S. Lewis, *Mere Christianity*, (New York: Touchstone, 1996), 121.

[INFLUENCED BY THE FEAR OF THE LORD]

The Bible talks about something called the fear of the Lord. Proverbs 1:7 says, "The fear of the Lord is the beginning of knowledge, but fools despise wisdom and instruction" (NKJV). It's important to understand that the fear of the Lord is completely different than the fear that flows from the kingdom of darkness. The fear of the Lord is actually part of love. It's fear of doing anything that would harm our relationship with Him. It's fear that comes from understanding the destructive consequences of sin on our lives. It is not the kind of fear that makes us run away from God, but draws us near to Him.

I love and fear cars, boats, and anything else that goes fast! Our family loves to go boating. As fun as it is, I have a healthy fear of that boat. If I don't respect it, things could get out of hand quickly and someone could get injured. In the same way, we were created to enjoy God, and to be in awe and wonder of Him.

God is love, and He is holy. While I get to enjoy His loving kindness and grace, I am also aware that I can't just do whatever I want in the name of grace. Sin has consequences. The reason we feel troubled inside when we sin is because our friend the Holy Spirit is working in us to bring us into our truest self—to help us let go of ways that contradict who we really are and be more like Jesus. His grace actually empowers us to live like He did—holy and pure.

What you fear is always connected to what you worship. In the Old Testament, God constantly warned Israel not to worship idols, because they would draw their hearts away from God. A modern-day idol is anything you have to check with before you obey God. Today, we worship what people think about us on social media, in our friend groups, or anything else that makes us feel good in the moment—and we wonder why our lives are like a yo-yo. When we dump that up-and-down life and embrace the fear of the Lord, the message of our lives begins to SPEAK of His grace and power.

When I first got saved, I had few options for worship music, but I wore them out. My heart got free when I locked myself in my room, danced upon my fears, and worshipped the Lord until His presence was the predominant Spirit influencing my life. Then, Hillsong came on the scene and gave language to the song of worship we were all feeling inside. Today, God is raising up a sound all over the earth through different worship expressions like Bethel Music, Jesus Culture, and others where we can draw near to God, be transformed in His presence, and learn the fear of the Lord.

The nature of God is love! Love doesn't control—it sets you free, empowers you, and reminds you of who you are when you feel lost. When you fear God, who is love, love is what you will receive, and freedom will be the result. The fear of God doesn't make God feel far away, but really close.

Fearing God is how we beat the fear of man. The fear of man looks like valuing other people's opinions over what God's Word says, and doing what they say. Pretty simple. Proverbs 29:25 says, "The fear of man brings a snare, but whoever trusts in the Lord shall be safe." I've never tried to trap an animal, but I know you catch one with bait. The bait that gets us to fall into the snare of the fear of man can look different for all of us, but it usually involves starting to listen to what others say about you more than God. If you've found yourself trapped—as I and every other believer have—grace is how we get out. Jesus is the only one who never got trapped. Yet He willingly put Himself in the trap by taking our place so we could go free. Just repent for putting man's opinions above God's and learn from it. Thank God for His Mercy and try again.

Have you ever tried to step out in faith and felt like you hit a wall—and the wall was what you imagined someone else might think of you? That's the fear of man. Jump anyways! Do it afraid and just move. Mark Twain said, "Courage is not the lack of fear. It's acting in spite of it."

The fear of man is not something you beat once in life. We need to keep our hearts before the Lord and keep His presence in the highest place of our hearts. The fear of the Lord keeps us true to who He says we are, and protects us from traps so our lives are free to SPEAK of His grace and power!

[THE FEAR OF GOD BRINGS PROTECTION]

I've been tempted many times to gossip about someone or talk badly about someone and felt the Holy Spirit tell me, "Sshhh." It was as though He was saying, "I love them. Please don't say that about them." It caused me to hold my tongue. I've also sensed the Holy Spirit telling me, "You don't need to be on the Internet right now. You're tired and don't want to see something that makes you feel dirty." So, I obey. The Holy Spirit protects me.

I've never had a porn problem since surrendering my life to Christ over twenty-one years ago, and it's because His presence in me rejects wanting anything like that. I closed that door permanently, and I know that opening it would destroy me and my family, and hurt a lot of other people. No way—not worth it! Because I closed that door, I don't even have a desire for it—it's not even a temptation. Sex in marriage is fulfilling, while porn is enslaving! The fear of God protects me, and protects what my life is speaking!

[THE FEAR OF THE LORD PURIFIES]

Bill Johnson says, "Love for God can be measure by what we hate." It's easy to hate the bad things that are happening around the world—but what about when you find something in you that's ugly? Proverbs 8:13 says, "All who fear the Lord will hate evil. Therefore, I hate pride and arrogance, corruption and perverse speech."

Years ago, when I was nineteen years old, I was jealous of a friend of mine because he was good at everything and had everything I wanted in life—favor, good looks, popularity, and more. One day, the Holy Spirit revealed my heart to me in a loving way. It felt gross to see what was in me. I hated what I saw. Not really knowing what I was doing, I lay down in my room in the form of a cross and said, "Jesus, Your Word says I am crucified with You. I repent for being jealous of my friend Ken and ask You to change me."

I didn't feel anything happen; in fact, I felt kind of silly. But I was willing to do whatever it took to see change in me.

A couple days later, I confessed my jealousy to Ken. He was gracious and cool about it, but the important thing was that something shifted in me. I was no longer jealous of him, and instead appreciated him. We are still great friends to this day. The Holy Spirit purified something that wasn't right in me and helped me become more of who I am, while removing a hindrance to our friendship.

The Holy Spirit is at work in our hearts. When I came to Christ at eighteen, my mind was filled with lust and images that warred against my soul and future. So, I read my Bible and prayed a lot till my thoughts were pure and my mind was clear. It was a process, but something in me wouldn't relent till my thoughts were pure. That is the fear of the Lord. Psalm 19:9 says, "The fear of the Lord is clean, enduring forever." The fear of the Lord purifies what our life is speaking!

[THE FEAR OF THE LORD WELCOMES FRIENDSHIP WITH GOD]

Every teenager and young adult is crying out for a friend who has got their back, knows how to keep a secret, and will unconditionally accept them. The problem is, most of your friends are not as awesome at being your friend as God is. Our relationship with God starts out getting to know Him as Savior, or maybe Deliverer and Healer. But as you set the highest place of your heart aside for Him alone, you will move into friendship with Him. Psalm 25:14 says, "The Lord is a friend to those who fear him. He teaches them his covenant" (NLT). It might sound offensive to suggest you might not already be friends with Jesus, but friendship is something you cultivate over time and by caring for what's important to the other person.

Years ago, I began to hear gossip about people that I perceived was true. The Holy Spirit said to me, "Can I trust you with people whom I love, who aren't perfect? Can I trust you to cover and pray for them without joining in on the gossip?" I sensed the Lord inviting me to love people whom He cares about in a greater way. He was showing me what friendship with Him looks like, which is to care for what's important to Him.

Invite the Holy Spirit to come and touch your heart afresh today. Pray something radical, like, "God I repent for fearing man, and look to You as my source for peace, joy, and fulfilment. Let the spirit of the fear of the Lord fill my life!"

I declare that the limitations that have been placed on you through the fickle opinions of others will fall off today as you draw near to the Lord! Set aside distractions, worship Him, and let the Holy Spirit renew your mind and heart till your life begins to SPEAK of who He says you are!

"WHEN YOUR LIFE IS MARKED BY AN ENCOUNTER WITH THE HOLY SPIRIT, YOU BECOME A CARRIER OF THAT ENCOUNTER FOR SOMEONE ELSE."

/ TOM CRANDALL

CHAPTER [3]

MARKED BY AN ENCOUNTER WITH THE HOLY SPIRIT

Growing up in Seattle, Washington, Jordan's life was filled with pain, loneliness, and heartache. After watching his dad get dragged from his house by a SWAT team, his summers were spent visiting his dad in prison. An influential family member told Jordan that he was probably gay, which led him into sexual confusion. Addicted to drugs and alcohol by the age of fifteen, Jordan's life was spinning out of control fast.

After seeing a friend's tweet about a special night at a local youth group in town, Jordan messaged him asking if he could come to the event. The friend picked him up and brought him to the youth service.

Jordan had never been to church before, so he really didn't know what he was getting himself into. From the moment he walked in the doors, he felt really uncomfortable, especially when they started singing songs and lifting their hands in the air. He was especially confused because they were singing to some guy named "Hosanna," and he just couldn't figure out who "Hosanna" was!

Finally, Jordan couldn't take it anymore, so he texted another friend and said, "Come get me now!" His friend showed up, but then became interested in what was going on and came up and sat on the front row. Jordan was freaking out and texting him, "Come on, let's get out of here!" But his friend was gripped by the Holy Spirit and didn't want to leave.

The youth pastor started speaking. Jordan began to feel like the pastor was talking directly to him, as if he was the only one in the room—especially when the man declared, "God has the power through Christ to break every chain, set you free from depression, and love you right where you are."

At the end of the message, the pastor asked if anyone wanted to surrender their life to Christ. Jordan's mind was still saying no, but his hand shot up. He walked forward, raised his hands, and felt love pour over him for the first time. He had an encounter with the love his heart had been searching for his entire life.

A few months later, Jordan attended a small group. The guys leading the group began describing radical encounters they had had with the Lord. Then they started talking about the "baptism in the Holy Spirit" and asked if anyone wanted this gift.

Jordan desperately wanted this encounter and said so. As the guys prayed for him, he felt fire pour over him from the top of his head, and felt like everything bad inside of him was draining out. Instantly, he started speaking in tongues for the first time.

Somebody in the group got a word of knowledge for back pain. One of the guys raised his hand and said, "That's me." Then the guy who had the word of knowledge said to Jordan, "Since you just got filled with the Holy Spirit, if you pray for this guy, he will be healed." When the man with back pain sat down, they noticed that one of his legs was shorter than the other. With his friends coaching him along, Jordan said, "Leg, grow in Jesus' name." Right in front of his eyes, the man's leg grew out! For the first time ever, Jordan saw someone get healed.

The next day, Jordan woke up and no longer desired his old life, or anything that used to give him joy. He was set on fire for God and wanted to pursue nothing but His presence. That encountered changed everything for Jordan. It showed him the love that had been chasing him down his whole life. He felt like he had finally stepped into who he was meant to be. He felt free, loved, and known. He felt like his life had value and that his destiny meant something. He was new! He went from abandoned to accepted, alone to comforted, and confused to seeing a powerful direction for his life. He was led out of sexual confusion into a life of love and peace that came from knowing the truth of how God designed him.

Jordan interned for me, and is now on our Young Saints leadership team. He has traveled with me and is incredible at leading people into a fresh encounter with God. I've watched him share his story. It's a testimony that releases so much hope and invites the presence of God to set free and heal others in broken situations. The Holy Spirit loves to rescue, restore, and love people.

[THE HOLY SPIRIT MAKES GOD PERSONAL, REAL, AND ALIVE]

Before I rededicated my life to Jesus as a teenager, I hated going to church. I thought it was boring and a waste of time. But after I encountered Jesus through the Holy Spirit, you couldn't keep me away from church. I wanted more of God!

There is no lack of good sermons, programs, and church services in America. Though these things are good and have their place, it's not how Jesus touched the world. I've heard truth in great sermons and been inspired in a lot of services, but nothing touches me deeper and leaves me more undone than a touch from the Holy Spirit. He is the one who makes Jesus come alive to us and empowers us to walk as Jesus did! Anyone who encounters the Holy Spirit is never the same!

The Holy Spirit is not some impersonal, mystical force. He is a person who lives in us. He is the most important person in my life, and I do my best to honor, listen to, and follow Him. He walks with me, helps me protect all of my relationships, never leaves me, guides me in wisdom, and empowers me for a life of faith and miracles.

The Bible reveals that God the Father, Jesus the Son, and the Holy Spirit are all equally God. Mario Murillo said, "There are three powers that bring men to God—the Father, the Son, and the Holy Spirit!"

The top priority of heaven in sending Jesus to the world was to reveal what God the Father looks like to an orphaned planet through the power of the Holy Spirit. Scripture reveals that Jesus is the exact image of the Father.[1] Bill Johnson says, "Jesus Christ is perfect theology. If you can't find it in the person of Jesus, it has reason to be questioned." But Jesus Christ not only revealed the Father—He also revealed what we were to look like and how we were to live as the Father's sons and daughters. He is our standard for life and ministry, and what He modeled for us is that we are to live 100 percent dependent upon the Holy Spirit. Though He was 100 percent God, He set aside the privileges of His divinity to become a man and show us what it looks like to live completely surrendered to the Holy Spirit. He was showing us how our lives

---

[1] Hebrews 1:3

are designed to operate when we receive His nature and His Spirit through being born again.

The Holy Spirit was so important to Jesus that He told His disciples they should rejoice that He was about to leave the earth, because then He could send the Holy Spirit to be with them and empower them to do even greater works than He did![2] He was basically saying, "Boys, what's been on me is about to get on you. Tag—you're it! Don't leave home till you receive what My Father promised!"

On the day of Pentecost, after waiting in prayer, unity, and worship for ten days, 120 people were baptized in the Holy Spirit and fire, and began speaking in tongues. As a result of this radical encounter, over 3,000 people were born again and baptized (immersed) in the Holy Spirit! This was the birthday of the church, and it looked like a wild party! The 120 were so impacted by the Holy Spirit that at first the crowd thought they were drunk! Their lives were speaking of a wild love encounter with God!

Everything in Scripture says that encounters with the Holy Spirit are not supposed to stop but only increase in our day. God is present here on earth as the Holy Spirit. The Holy Spirit is the active agent of God on the earth to do the will of the Father through Christ Jesus the Son. He is how we connect with God the Father and Jesus the Son. If we don't have a connection with the Holy Spirit, we don't have a connection with God.

Benny Hinn says, "If you're wondering what the Holy Spirit is like, He's like Jesus without flesh. He's just like Him." He can be trusted. Even if He is doing something in us that stretches us, He can be trusted to do all things well. When the Holy Spirit is living in us, He uses everyday life, struggles, victories, and even failure to make us more like

---

[2] John 14:12, 16:7-9

Jesus. He is a gracious friend, and comforting companion, and He is faithful to lead us in truth and freedom.

Years ago, while I was still living at home with my parents, before anyone had a cell phone, we had landline telephones! You could have several phones in the house but they were all connected to one line. At times, I would be on the phone with a friend, and my brother would pick up another phone in the house and start yelling at me—loud enough for my friend to hear—to get off the phone. It was embarrassing and aggravating! The old Tom wanted to kill him, but the Holy Spirit was in me helping me forgive and find a better way to respond than in anger. He helped me live out my faith in everyday life.

As a new believer, I often sat in my living room and read my Bible. I didn't understand most of what I read, but then certain things would leap off the page and touch me. At the time I just thought I was really excited, but later I discovered it was the Holy Spirit who was talking to me and helping me develop a relationship with Him through His Word.

The Holy Spirit convicts the world of sin, then points them to Jesus the Savior. He reveals the Father, who heals our hearts and gives us comfort. And He empowers believers to live like Jesus and demonstrate the heart of the Father. Religion always tries to remove the Holy Spirit from the church's corporate expression in order to make us more palatable for the world. This is an error, because the world can't even see Jesus without the power of the Holy Spirit. He loves going with you into fifth period, showing up to heal your friends, and demonstrating the love of the Father! He is the greatest tangible gift humanity has ever received!

[THE HOLY SPIRIT IS MOVING ALL OVER THE PLANET]

Several years ago, we were having a night at our youth service called a "friend night," where we designed the whole service around kids encountering God for the first time. During worship, I heard the Holy Spirit whisper in my thoughts, "Shin splints." Later, as I was giving my message, I declared, "Nothing is impossible for the person who puts their faith in Jesus Christ!" The very next thought that came to my mind was, "Shin splints." So, I asked the crowd of about 250 kids, "Who here has shin splints?" One young man raised his hand. He said his pain level was a seven on a scale of one to ten. Then I declared, "God is about to heal you." Right then and there, I had his friends put their hands on him and I prayed a ten-second prayer. Afterwards, he checked his legs and freaked out. He said his pain level was a one... no half... nothing! He gave his life to Christ that night, along with about fifty other kids. I later discovered that was his first time ever going to church. He didn't even own a Bible and he came to youth group high on marijuana!

What does this encounter say about God? When we see a crowd, He sees an individual whom He simply loves and desires to know. He chose the least likely person and revealed Himself to him. This young man's encounter with God was personal, loving, and powerful because the Holy Spirit specifically called him out and healed him. He was never the same again, and neither were we!

God is pouring out the Holy Spirit all over the earth, and we get to be a part of it! In the Middle East and other regions where there is no church, Jesus is revealing Himself to Muslims in dreams, and thousands are coming to Christ as a result. In China, thousands get saved every day. In Europe, many of our friends are leading a movement—Europe Shall Be Saved—and thousands are filling stadiums and being marked by encounters. In Russia, there is a hunger that is sweeping thousands into the kingdom. God is moving in Africa, Australia, and on every continent on the globe.

But it is also America's time! With racial tension still a reality, gender confusion, cyber bullying, and gross sexual immorality at our fingertips more than ever before, now is the time for a fresh outpouring of the Holy Spirit to reveal the Father through Christ. Historically, God always shows up in dark times, and young people are always part of the movements He sparks to bring transformation! Politics has its place, but isn't going to heal anything. We need God! On the day of Pentecost, the Holy Spirit brought men together in unity like no campaign or protest ever could. Even America was marked by an encounter with the Holy Spirit in the First and Second Great Awakenings. The Azusa Street Revival, led by a black man named William Seymour, released power that spoke a message of hope and redemption to the world and brought down walls of division and racial segregation. It's time for a fresh outpouring of the Holy Spirit!

The Holy Spirit is the gift the Father promised. We receive Him by coming like a child and simply asking Him to come. He comes the way He wants to when we ask Him to come. The Prince of Peace is also the Lion of the Tribe of Judah. He can't be reduced to a mere formula to fit our lives. He is an all-consuming fire! If it was legal in the Bible, it's legal now. Be filled with the Holy Spirit! You will SPEAK in tongues, have visions and dreams, walk in purity and power, and your life will begin to SPEAK of Jesus in such a way that your friends will say of you as people said of the disciples: "Now when they saw the boldness of Peter and John, and perceived that they were uneducated and untrained men, they marveled.

And they realized that they had been with Jesus."[3]

Watching Jesus is how we learn how to walk with the Holy Spirit. Jesus talked about the good news of the kingdom of God, then released encounters:

> And Jesus went about all Galilee, teaching in their synagogues, preaching the gospel of the kingdom, and healing all kinds of sickness and all kinds of disease among the people. Then His fame went throughout all Syria; and they brought to Him all sick people who were afflicted with various diseases and torments, and those who were demon-possessed, epileptics, and paralytics; and He healed them. Great multitudes followed Him...[4]

Everyone who encountered Jesus was healed, set free and touched at their greatest point of need. He became famous for it, and word of mouth spread in such a way that thousands came from all over to receive from Him. There was no Instagram or Facebook—just power and love that made people's lives better. They had more to talk about than how good the sermon was. They talked about how loved and liberated they felt. Therefore, thousands came!

How is it today that we let "good ministry" replace releasing encounters with Jesus?

I've seen trends come and go in churches, but all the necessary planning in the world doesn't make up for our lack of power and encounters that we—and all people—are really hungry for. We must let our encounters with Jesus be what our lives are speaking!

---

[3] Acts 4:13
[4] Matthew 4:23

[CARRIER OF AN ENCOUNTER]

When you have an encounter, you become the carrier of an encounter for someone else!

Years ago, I went on a mission trip to Thailand and ate something I had never seen in America before: sweet sticky rice and mangos. If you've never had it before, it will set you free at another level! You dig the sticky rice out of a deep bowl, form it with your hands into rice tongs, then pick up the mango with it and the down the hatch it goes! Ah! I can taste it now! You want some?

That's how the kingdom of God works—except better! Just as your physical senses were awakened to what I just described, when you describe how Jesus touched your life, His presence fills the space and He is ready to do the same miracle you just talked about! It's called the power of the testimony, and it is how the Holy Spirit moves to build faith and create moments for Him to reveal Jesus. Revelation 19:10 says, "The testimony of Jesus is the spirit of prophecy." Prophecy simply means to declare what God is saying and doing. When you release a testimony, it gives hope and truth with power to do the same miracle that was just declared.

When you release an encounter, more encounters are available. We are constantly sharing testimonies of what God is doing at Young Saints, and most of the time after a testimony is shared I will ask, "Who needs what God did in their life?" This gives people a chance to respond, which brings more breakthrough. After big events like Young Saints Youth Camp or Young Saints Youth Conference, we will worship the Lord and then just have kids share testimonies of what the Lord did at the event. Every time, more kids get touched by God as a result. It is so fun and powerful!

[CUTTING SCARS REMOVED]

On the first night of our Young Saints Youth Camp in 2016, I made the following declaration before we started worship: "Cutting scars from self-harm are going to vanish off of people's bodies this week!" Later, I found out that scars supernaturally vanished from a girl's arms!

The next Sunday night after Youth Camp, I opened the service at Bethel Church with this testimony. Later that night, a teenager came up to me with her friends. They were all freaking out because her scars were noticeably lighter. A month later, her deep red scars were completely gone, with only slight marring of the surface of the skin that you couldn't see unless you really looked. This girl felt so loved and known by Jesus that it started a deep healing process in her heart. She got baptized in the Holy Spirit and started speaking in tongues and having visions and dreams. She was overjoyed in her relationship with Jesus and became a walking encounter! Her life SPEAKS loudly of Jesus and how He touched her life.

I shared this testimony at Young Saints, only to find out that one of our girls had scars all over the front of her thighs that vanished that night as well as a result of hearing the testimony!

In our Bethel School of Supernatural Ministry, we send over 2,000 people around the world on mission trips. Some of our students heard me sharing these testimonies, took them to South Africa, and saw scars removed on their trip!

I've lost count of how many encounters people have had with Jesus the Healer that started with one declaration and sharing the testimony of what He had done.

What has marked your life is what your life is speaking.

When you get marked by an encounter with God, and recognize the Holy Spirit, you will begin to burn with heaven's fuel!

[HOW TO HAVE A FRESH ENCOUNTER]

I've had encounters where I felt like I had been hit like a freight train from heaven—they were impossible to miss. But most of the time, the Holy Spirit whispers to my heart. Both encounters are powerful and necessary, and all are valuable. One encounter doesn't discount another.

I have been married for eighteen years to my best friend and the most beautiful woman I know. Every encounter with her is important to me because of who she is in my life. I love her. It's the same with the Holy Spirit. Encountering God starts with Him pursuing us. He touches us, we recognize that it's Him, and then respond by pursuing Him.

God is huge, and encountering Him can't be narrowed down to a few simple steps. However, the Bible does give us some important direction on what we can do to encounter Him.

[PRAYER AND WORSHIP]

Jesus taught us how to pray in Matthew 6:5-15. Prayer is communication with God and how we learn to be in His presence. It's where we receive what we are all craving—to be known and loved. It's how we build a friendship with the Holy Spirit that will last through every season and challenge we face.

Corrie Ten Boom was a survivor of the Holocaust and a believer who asked, "Is prayer your steering wheel or your spare tire?" There has never been a time when more is competing for our attention. We live so mentally cluttered and distracted that it becomes challenging to give God space. Turn off your iPhone and remove the clutter. Get alone in your room or the place you feel most connected to God. You could either be in silence or have your favorite worship music playing. Then start a conversation. The best place to start is with being thankful! A heart of gratitude and thanksgiving will inoculate you from the demonic, self-absorbed life the enemy wants to trip you with, and release you into encounters that will fuel the fire of God in your heart.

There is nothing more exhilarating than becoming friends with God, and it happens because you take the time to develop a relationship! Nothing replaces spending time alone with God. Most of the time when I get anxious and worried about something, it is due to a lack of prayer. I pray and read my Bible most mornings before checking social media, news, or emails so that He sets the tone for my day, not the clutter.

We were designed for worship, and to receive life from what we worship. Worship means to bow down and kiss towards. Everyone worships something, whether it's God, a sports team, a boyfriend, or whatever you put in the "God spot" of your heart. If we worship anything besides God, we will have limited strength, and believe lies that release fear and torment. But if we worship God, we will receive the unlimited and immeasurable life of God. When we worship the Healer, we will have access to healing. When we worship the Savior, we receive saving grace. When we worship Jesus, we have access to all that He is! All the sermons in the world pale in comparison to His matchless wonder, which we can experience when we set aside time to pray and worship the Lord.

[THE BIBLE]

Read this next line slowly: Jesus *is* the Word of God, and the Bible is where you'll find Him.

When I don't know what God is saying, I read what He said until I start to hear Him. Many of us are waiting to get "zapped" so we can say we had an encounter, when most of the time it looks as simple as God speaking to us through His Word. When I first started reading my Bible, I was hungry to know God. I didn't always understand what I was reading, but I kept reading till things leapt off the page and came alive. The Holy Spirit is waiting to talk to you about your life as you give attention to what He said in Scripture. He makes the Word of God come alive to reveal Jesus to you personally! It's what He loves to do!

To receive the full impact of an encounter in the Word, you have to do what it says. James 1:22-24 says: "But don't just listen to God's word. You must do what it says. Otherwise, you are only fooling yourselves. For if you listen to the word and don't obey, it is like glancing at your face in a mirror. You see yourself, walk away, and forget what you look like" (NLT).

[COMMUNITY]

I used to live in Salt Lake City, Utah, which is a beautiful city surrounded by mountains. One day, some military personnel were doing some training in the mountains when a spark from a machine gun ignited a fire. It got out of hand so fast that they couldn't get it under control and put it out. The fire burned up the side of the mountain, crested on the top for the whole city to see, and released smoke that began to fill the entire valley. We watched all day as the fire consumed the entire mountainside. While watching the fire, it was as if the Holy Spirit was saying to me, "This is how I've called My people to burn." He wants our passion and love for God and one another to be visible to entire cities.

None of us can burn alone for very long. A hot coal in a fire only remains hot by staying in the fire. In the same way, we stay on fire for Jesus by staying connected to others who are pursuing and encountering Him. As important as it is to consistently attend a local church, the deeper purpose of community is to let others into our lives and encounter God together with them, just as the disciples did when they received the Holy Spirit.

We have a group of kids at Young Saints who just started getting together on Friday nights to worship and share life together. These kids are a thermostat in our city, carrying the Holy Spirit everywhere they go. They are keeping their fire hot by staying in community with each other and pursuing God together.

Encounters with the Holy Spirit change everything! It's time to burn and let our lives SPEAK of what He is doing on the planet. When our friends, sports teams, social media pages, and family see us and how the Holy Spirit has made us bold, they will take note that we have been with Jesus!

"

BELIEFS ARE SHAPED FROM 1 OF 2 WORLDS

TRUTH OR LIES

"

TOM CRANDALL
#YOURLIFESPEAKS

CHAPTER [4]

BELIEF SHAPES HISTORY

R andy is a friend of mine who coaches football. Several years ago, I suggested that he read a book called *Victorious Mindsets* by Steve Backlund. It's a wonderful book that has impacted my own life in a drastic way. While I *did* think Randy would read the book and grow in his beliefs about God and himself, I *didn't* know it would have such a massive impact on his entire community!

Randy coached a "C" football team of eighth-graders called the Riverton Silverwolves. These were the young men who not only "didn't make the team"—they didn't even make the backup team! You can imagine that the morale of Randy's team had every reason to be low right from the start. However, Randy saw this as an opportunity to practice what he had learned from *Victorious Mindsets.* During every football practice, he had his players declare that they were champions. Every Friday night, his players had to memorize a verse from the Bible if they wanted to play in the game the next day. That verse was Philippians 4:13, which says, "I can do all things through Christ who strengthens me."

Because the players and coaches started training their minds to believe they were champions, they actually started expecting to have a good season! By the time the first game kicked off, hopes were high. And then... they lost. Not only did they lose their first game 47-0, they went on to lose the next three games by an average of 36 points!

What happened to "being a champion"? The team certainly didn't *feel* like champions with a 0-4 start to the season. The parents of the players started complaining and questioning Randy's coaching ability and methods, and the players started to get teased and called names at school.

Randy realized his players and fellow coaches were losing all hope. At times, he felt like he was the only person who believed they still had a chance of winning that season. On the brink of losing his entire team to disunity and division, Randy and the other coaches had a conversation with the players.

"Guys, we have to be okay when we get knocked down, but we don't have to stay down!" Randy exhorted his guys. "We don't have to accept being losers. Losers are people who quit. If you learn to never quit, you'll never be a loser! You have two choices. You can either quit trying—and you know what you will be called if you do (a loser)—or you can get back up and learn to do hard things, like practice hard this week and get a win this Saturday. Who's in?"

The team went back to practice, declaring their identity as champions, and ending each practice with their war cry: "Victorious Mindset!"

When the Silverwolves took the field for their next game, they won in overtime. The explosion of joy that followed was breathtaking. Parents, coaches, and players alike were screaming and jumping up and down with excitement. They had finally tasted the victory they had been believing for.

But it didn't stop there. The Riverton Silverwolves went on to win three of their next four games and found themselves in the playoffs. The champion mentality of the players and coaches continued to help them dominate the competition, and before they knew it, Randy's team found themselves heading to the championship game.

At game time, the Silverwolves marched into the packed-out coliseum, ready to go to battle. Even though the other team—the West Jordan "A" team—was highly favored to win, Randy and his fellow coaches knew their boys had it in them to do something incredible. The first whistle blew, helmets and pads cracked and collided, and fans and family cheered and screamed.

The Silverwolves played valiantly, but so did their opponent, and when half-time came the two teams were tied. Randy talked to his men in the locker room, encouraging them and charging them up. Then he and his coaches walked back onto the sidelines, leaving the players by themselves in the locker room. After gazing across the field, looking up at the scoreboard, and soaking in the rich moment of being at the championship game, Randy looked back towards the locker room and smiled. *This is it*, he thought. *This is where we find out if they really do have a victorious mindset. Do they really believe what the coaches and I have been telling them all season long?*

When the Silverwolves emerged from the locker room, they were chanting a battle cry and boiling over with passion. They had come to win. And they did just that. When the dust settled and the clock hit zero, Randy's "C team" boys had won the championship 47-21. Their victorious mindsets had defined their reality.

When Randy told me this story, I was blown away. Because one man decided to change the way he thought about God and himself, his example and teaching inspired a team of young men to accomplish something no one (including themselves) thought they could achieve.

[THE POWER OF BELIEF]

What you believe about yourself will SPEAK in ways you never knew possible. Our beliefs shape the course of our lives, and declare to the world what our lives are speaking! Look at every powerful movie or story out there, from *Braveheart* to *The Hunger Games*, *Remember the Titans*, and *The Avengers*. Someone believed against all odds and prevailed in the end.

Beliefs are the door to the spirit realm, which is why it's vital to believe truth about who God is and who we are. Beliefs that are true open the door to courage, love, justice, and grace.

Dr. Martin Luther King Jr.'s beliefs are still preaching today, perhaps even louder than when he lived. His beliefs and the bold love that flowed from him killed the lie that people of color are subject to the white man. His beliefs turned into actions and he became the catalyst for cultural transformation. Today, we get to stand on his shoulders because he didn't waver from his beliefs.

Though truth will prevail in the end, people still wrestle with demonic beliefs of racism. God help us. It's obvious that as believers we are in a war, but unless we are aware of the battle or our real enemy, we either won't fight, or we'll fight the wrong enemy using the wrong strategies. *The battle we are fighting isn't good vs. evil, or even light vs. darkness. It is truth vs. lies.*

People engage in self-harm by cutting themselves. They believe they will be able to release the pain in their hearts, only to discover that they just made it worse. Others attempt suicide because they believe things would be easier if they were gone, not realizing suicide is a permanent solution to a temporary problem. Self-harm can even look like getting married in a rush against sound counsel and red flags. Some people believe the relationship in front of them is the only potential relationship they will have in their lifetime. Rushing into a covenant can result in a life marked with pain.

Bill Johnson says, "When we believe a lie, we empower the liar." The truth is, the liar has been defeated by Jesus, and the only power he has over us is when our beliefs partner with his lies. We do this by entertaining those lies in our thoughts and imagination. Have you ever had an imaginary conversation with another person and found yourself getting mad or offended at them? At times, we imagine things going wrong and believe the worst about another person. Then when we see them, we feel like it really happened. Our thoughts and imagination essentially led us into agreement with a false belief, and that belief became a lens through which we started to interpret reality. This is why Paul tells us to "take every thought captive to obey Christ."[1] Otherwise, bad thoughts will produce bad beliefs, which will produce bad actions.

Truth isn't a set of beliefs, creed, or doctrine. It's ultimate reality—the reality of God. Specifically, Truth is a person named Jesus. The Bible reveals Him perfectly and declares that He never changes. Before Jesus went to the cross, He said to Pontius Pilate, "Everyone who is of the truth hears My voice." Pilate said to Him, "What is truth?"[2] Jesus never responded because Pilate was looking at it. That's crazy if you stop and think about it. Read about Jesus in the Bible, for that is where we find Truth! He's with us always. My belief that He's always with me opens the door for me to recognize Him in every situation.

---

[1] 2 Corinthians 10:5 ESV
[2] John 18:38-38

Any event, past, present, or future, in which we don't see God at work is where the enemy seeks to establish a stronghold of bad beliefs about God and who we are. For example, God's Word says, "Never will I leave you; never will I forsake you,"[3] so we have the legal right to walk with the belief that we have never been, nor will be, alone. When we go through a difficult time or face disappointment, we have a choice to believe lies or truth. Whichever one we partner with will be the spirit released, and the stronghold we establish in our thoughts.

Truth releases hope.

Lies release hopelessness.

Steve Backlund says, "Hopelessness about a problem is a bigger problem than the problem." Why? Because hopelessness, anxiety, and fear signal that somewhere we are believing a lie. And until we stop believing a lie, it will be practically impossible to find a solution to a problem. Have you ever noticed that when you feel hopeful, it becomes easier to see solutions, and when you're discouraged you don't even want to try? It's time to get our hopes up!

One day in a Bethel staff meeting, Bill Johnson taught us something so powerful on this subject. He explained that a thought rooted in a lie is like a brick. The enemy seeks to establish lie upon a lie, brick upon brick, in our thoughts, until we have built a stronghold or fortress in our minds where the enemy can come and go. The same principle applies to building a stronghold of truth. We were designed to partner with truth through our thoughts, so the Lord becomes the stronghold in our minds where the Holy Spirit can come and flow. When the Lord becomes the stronghold in our thought life, our lives will SPEAK *life and peace.*

---

[3] Hebrews 13:5 NIV

Thank God that Dr. King didn't believe the lie that God abandoned him in the midst of the death threats and difficulty he faced. In his last speech, he said, "We've got some difficult days ahead. But it really doesn't matter with me now because I've been to the mountaintop... I've looked over and I've seen the promised land. I may not get there with you. But I want you to know tonight that we as a people will get to the promised land."[4] The legacy of hope Dr. King left continues to SPEAK in this generation.

Dr. King stayed true in the most intense opposition a man could face. He never lost his conviction to love his enemies, and he did so in such a powerful way that it released grace for them to change. His life will speak for the rest of time because his beliefs matched heaven's truth with extreme courage in the face of fear.

You can step into freedom by breaking up with lies and making an agreement with truth. This is how you move from depression to joy, hopelessness to hope, and stuck to moving forward. We do this through belief in Jesus that leads to action.

What makes belief powerful is the object of the belief. *Belief in Jesus is so powerful* that the woman who "had suffered for twelve years with constant bleeding" said in her heart, "If I can just touch his robe, I will be healed."[5] When she touched the Lord, He felt power leave Him and she was immediately made whole.

Another time, Jesus healed ten men who had leprosy. When one came back to thank Jesus, the Lord said, "Arise, go your way. Your faith has made you well."[6]

---

[4] Dr. Martin Luther King, Jr. "I've Been to the Mountaintop," delivered April 3, 1968.

[5] Matthew 9:20-21 NLT

[6] Luke 17:19

Another time, a centurion who had a sick servant told the Lord: "'I am not worthy that You should come under my roof. But only *speak* a word, and my servant will be healed'... Then Jesus said to the centurion, 'Go your way; and as you have believed, so let it be done for you.' And his servant was healed that same hour."[7]

How is the Holy Spirit leading you today to align your beliefs with heaven?

[TEARING DOWN STRONGHOLDS OF BAD BELIEFS]

Because of the finished work on the cross, we stand already victorious. Everything we are fighting for has already been paid for by Jesus, and we are on a journey of renewing our minds to become what He already says we are.

The Bible shows us how to cast down lies and step into truth in 2 Corinthians 10:3-5:

> For though we live in the world, we do not wage war as the world does. The weapons we fight with are not the weapons of the world. On the contrary, they have divine power to demolish strongholds. We demolish arguments and every pretension that sets itself up against the knowledge of God, and we take captive every thought to make it obedient to Christ. (NIV)

One day, I was battling hopelessness about a situation in my life. I knew I was believing a lie I couldn't see, so I got alone for a morning and began to lift my voice in worship, giving thanks to God for always being with me, never leaving me, and working all things together for my good and His glory.

---

[7] Matthew 8:8, 13, my emphasis

To be honest, it was really hard because my feelings were telling me to quit, that nothing would change, and that it would just be easier to blame someone for what I was going through. I remember making a choice to agree with the psalmist, King David, in Psalm 34:1-6:

> I will bless the LORD at all times;
>
> His praise shall continually be in my mouth.
>
> My soul shall make its boast in the LORD;
>
> The humble shall hear of it and be glad.
>
> Oh, magnify the LORD with me,
>
> And let us exalt His name together.
>
> I sought the LORD, and He heard me,
>
> And delivered me from all my fears.
>
> They looked to Him and were radiant,
>
> And their faces were not ashamed.
>
> This poor man cried out, and the LORD heard him,
>
> And saved him out of all his troubles.

David wrote this following a really hard time, when he was facing possible death! I read it out loud for my soul to hear, until God was accurately bigger than my little problem.

We don't tear down strongholds by thinking about them, but by *SPEAKING* to them! The "weapons of our warfare" come from our own tongue! I have found that if what is in my mouth doesn't edify me, I need to be quiet and join a voice like David's that will shift something in me to align with heaven's beliefs about me.

My feelings don't drive my beliefs—my beliefs drive my feelings!

[SING, DANCE, AND SHOUT FOR THE VICTORY]

Another way to pull down strongholds is through radical praise! Psalm 22:3 says, "But You are holy, enthroned in the praises of Israel." When you exalt the Lord and His attributes, counteracting the lie with the truth of who He is, you demolish strongholds that produce discouragement and establish the stronghold of the Lord that releases hope. The battle for our freedom has already been won. When Jesus rose from the grave, He rendered the powers of darkness completely defeated. We don't fight for victory, but from a place of victory. When we lift our whole being to the Lord, moving our bodies and lifting our hands and voices in response to His victory, our minds will clearly see the reality of who He is. Jesus, our victor, will invade our lives through our beliefs!

[SPEAK AND BELIEVE TOGETHER]

Lastly, as we learned from Randy and his football team—they fought and believed together! Like a red-hot coal in a fire with other coals, we were never meant to burn alone. We can't let fear tell us to be quiet, but must courageously run at fear, stepping into the light with our friends and family. There isn't much we can win alone, but nothing is impossible if we fight together!

Fear is a liar, and will always tell you you're alone and the only one with this problem. Like a bad poker player, the devil has overplayed his hand. If we don't get this we will live frustrated. The enemy is a defeated foe who seeks to trip us on the inside using the outward circumstances of life that we all face. His ultimate goal is to shut down the power of God that wants to flow through us. The kingdom of God lives inside us to shift circumstances around us through our beliefs. We release our faith through the words we speak, the songs we sing, the prayers we pray, and the bold steps we take to trust and obey the voice of the Holy Spirit.

The Holy Spirit is like a flashlight inside a believer. He spots lies like Indiana Jones spots a trap in a deep, dark cave! I have found myself in the caverns of life when Holy Spirit put His flashlight on my fears, exposing the silly stronghold in my thoughts. When I whipped the lie I was believing with truth, the stronghold came down like a house of cards.

When our beliefs about God line up with truth, the result will be a life of freedom, joy, and peace. Jesus said, "If you hold to my teaching, you are really my disciples. Then you will know the truth, and the truth will set you free."[8]

No matter how much darkness a person is sitting in, or how long you have believed lies, truth has power to set anyone free, because truth is not a set of rules or a standard to attain—Truth is a person and His name is Jesus. Believing truth means seeing Jesus accurately for who He is, and inviting Him into your circumstances. The Bible reveals that Jesus was more than a good man, a prophet, or a healer—He was God in the flesh. God looks like Jesus and God never changes. Jesus loves us, and as long as there is breath in our lungs, there is mercy that will triumph over all judgement in our lives.

[BECOMING PEOPLE OF BIG BELIEFS]

In the summer of 2010, I was a youth pastor in Salt Lake City. I had come to Jesus Culture conferences and had been reading books from Bethel for a while. At one point, I told my wife, "I could never be a youth pastor for anyone else unless it was Bill Johnson." Little did I know that God was

[8] John 8:31-32 NIV

speaking through my desires. I had been receiving from Bill for around five to six years, and my heart was fixed on what he was going after—revival and the presence of God at any cost.

Then I had a dream where I introduced Bill to our church. When he was done speaking, he walked out of the church and I followed him. As soon as we stepped out of the back doors of the church, we were instantly in Bethel's bookstore. The dream felt very real, and I felt the presence of God, so I ended up sharing it with my pastor on a Friday night after the prayer meeting. Little did I know that Banning Liebscher, the director of Jesus Culture, had called him the same day asking for permission to interview me to possibly be Bill Johnson's next youth pastor. After interviewing on Skype and flying out to Redding, we met with Bill, Kris, and Danny all in one day, and at the end of the interview process, they hired us! I was floored and my faith was soaring. I received a confidence and strength in my heart that God was leading me, knew me, and was working out all things for my good and His glory. He's such a good Father and leads us through His voice with great love—but it comes through our belief and faith in who He is.

Romans 15:13 says, "Now may the God of hope fill you with all joy and peace in *believing*, that you may abound in hope by the power of the Holy Spirit."

The voice we hear is what we live from and what our lives are speaking. Belief and faith grow from the voice of God that we hear and becomes the source from which we live. God hasn't just called us to move mountains with faith; He wants our joy to overflow because we are doing it out of relationship with our Father. Unless our beliefs are rooted in living from the voice of God, we risk creating a supernatural religion of form without power. The greatest Encourager lives inside us! Jesus, the greatest Savior, Healer, and Deliverer, lives in us through His Holy Spirit. He is guiding our lives on this great adventure called life, transforming us to look more like Him through our faith.

God wants to strengthen our lives and bless us through His voice as we walk with Him. Big faith always starts small like a seed. Discounting what you have aborts growth, usually on the altar of comparison. The Bible says in Romans 12:3 that "God has dealt to each one a measure of faith." If Christ is in you, then you have faith, because He's who our faith is in. Getting lost in worship, giving thanks and exalting Him with your own lips, and then acting on His voice is how you grow the seed of faith within you. You can grow your beliefs today by hearing His voice through His Word, your dreams, the still small voice, and prophetic words from other believers. The voice of God is an invitation into this great adventure, in which the kingdom of this world becomes the kingdom of our God through our beliefs.

[NOTHING HAPPENS UNTIL YOU FIRST MAKE A DECLARATION]

Heaven is waiting to break into our lives through the partnerships we make with our words and beliefs. Proverbs 18:21 says, "Death and life are in the power of the tongue, and those who love it will eat its fruit." When Jesus declared on the cross, "It is finished," He was announcing that the price for our salvation, redemption, healing, and future had been fully paid for. Our declarations are connected to the unseen realm of what He paid for. When we speak, we align ourselves to receive what heaven paid for through our beliefs and faith. Faith is a gift that Jesus paid for, not something we earn through works.

Paul the apostle taught the believers in Rome that "faith comes by hearing, and hearing by the word of God."[9] "Word" here is the Greek word *rhema,* which means something said, a saying or statement. This implies that when we SPEAK truth over our lives, our faith grows in what is spoken.

Our lives will speak what we speak over ourselves. If we speak rejection, we will believe rejection, and get rejected. If we speak acceptance, we will believe acceptance, and get accepted. We can SPEAK powerful declarations over our lives and form the right beliefs through any situation we face.

The Bible calls us "believers," not "feelers." Though feelings are valuable, they are not the primary thing that leads us. We are not subject to our feelings as believers—we have the power to shift things through a declaration! Romans 10:8-10 says:

> *The word is near you, in your mouth and in your heart"* (that is, the word of faith which we preach): that if you confess with your mouth the Lord Jesus and *believe* in your heart that God has raised Him from the dead, you will be saved. For with the heart one *believes* unto righteousness, and with the mouth confession is made unto salvation.

These powerful verses show you how you can meet Christ right now through faith! Just do what it says—declare His lordship over your life and start walking with Jesus.

Our friend Randy spoke "Victorious Mindsets" over his own life, which became what his life began to SPEAK. He had supernatural grace to lead his team through great difficulty all the way to victory, because the whole team began to SPEAK what his life spoke. This brought great breakthrough for the community. Their declarations opened the door to courage from the unseen realm that they didn't presently have, and turned the losers into champions!

What declarations do you need to SPEAK over your life today? Try these:

- I can do all things through Christ who gives me strength. (Philippians 4:13)

- Nothing is impossible for those who believe. (Mark 9:23)

- I am perfected in love and have great boldness, because as He is, so am I in this world. (1 John 4:17)

- I was made for the voice of God! (John 10)

- The same Spirit that raised Christ from the dead lives in me! (Romans 8:11)

- I am no longer a sinner, but a saint who is set apart for love, to walk in friendship with God and carry His glory!

- My life SPEAKS of the grace and mercy of Jesus.

- I will let my life SPEAK!

—

The *voice* you let
shape you will be
the *voice* that

SPEAKS
through you.

TOM CRANDALL

CHAPTER [5]

WHEN GOD SPEAKS

Natalie was a bright fifteen-year-old whose spirit walked with a limp. Her world had been rocked with pain when her dad died on August thirteenth. Every year since, this day was an unwelcome anniversary with pain and confusion. She did her best to pick herself up. She strove to do life well, grow up, and be who she was supposed to be.

During the summer of 2015, Natalie went to Young Saints Youth Camp. One of the guest speakers, Shawn Bolz, was getting really specific words of knowledge for people. He was calling out names, birthdays, parents' names, and other specific things that only God could have known. More than anything, Natalie wanted to hear from God. She wanted to know that the Holy Spirit was desiring to work in her heart. She just knew that if Shawn Bolz had a word of knowledge about her father's death, it would bring healing. She closed her eyes, and said a silent but desperate prayer: *God, let him call out August thirteenth.* It didn't happen.

Several months later, she signed up for our student leadership team. To join the team, students must participate in a weekend retreat. The night she was supposed to leave for the retreat, Natalie sat in her room, debating whether or not she should go. She knew there would probably be words of knowledge. Was she setting herself up for another disappointment? Did God want to touch her tonight? Would someone say the words "August thirteenth"? Finally, with questions and doubts still racing through her mind, Natalie stood and walked towards her bedroom door. She was going to the retreat. She wasn't going to let fear stop her from chasing the encounter with God that she longed for.

That night, several teenagers were given the opportunity to SPEAK words of knowledge over their peers. One of them called out a date: *August thirteenth.* Natalie was overwhelmed with emotion as she joyfully announced to her friends the significance of the date. God had answered her cry for a touch from heaven. Everyone gathered around her to pray for her. Doubts, confusion, discouragement, and pain were instantly lifted off her in a moment, and faith filled her heart. Natalie felt known by God—seen by her Father.

[HOW WE HEAR GOD]

God is always SPEAKING. He's never silent. Many times, the reason we don't hear Him is because of a bad belief that He's not talking, or has abandoned us for some reason. But even in your worst moment, God still SPEAKS and is with you. "For He Himself has said, *"I will never leave you nor forsake you."*[1]

The voice we think is God shapes what our lives SPEAK, because the way God SPEAKS to us is the way He SPEAKS through us. If we hear a condemning, judgmental God, we will sound like a condemning, judgmental Christian. If we hear a loving and gracious Father, that is what the world around us will hear us SPEAK.

As a new believer, I used to really struggle hearing the voice of God. Where I was raised, there was a lot of

[1] Hebrews 13:5

misunderstanding on this topic, and it seemed like many people were more afraid of getting deceived than they wanted to hear from God. I don't ever remember it being something that was talked about or celebrated, which left me to figure it out for myself. Even so, God was faithful to SPEAK.

Bobby Conner said, "God has more power to direct us than the devil does to deceive us." I used to confess over myself, "I just don't hear the voice of God," "I struggle hearing His voice," or, "He talks to everyone else more clearly than He talks to me." My bad beliefs about the voice of God turned into a declaration that shaped how I experienced His voice. The lies I believed were a bigger problem than any problem I was facing. My beliefs were driving me with fear and anxiety, rather than leading me with joy and peace.

Fear drives us, but love leads us. We can let bad beliefs fall off today, and let all the other voices be silenced as we step into the river of His grace, where He is SPEAKING.

[RECOGNIZING WHO IS SPEAKING]

One day, after I had just taken the job as youth pastor at Bethel, a voice came to me when I was getting ready for work that said, "You have missed it coming here. God is not happy with you." Thankfully, I recognized this voice as the enemy's and this tactic as the old "bully in the seventh-grade hallway" approach, trying to intimidate me and get me to open the door to fear in my life. In my mind's eye, I turned towards the voice and faced it as I said, "I recognize you." Then it began to SPEAK hopeless lies like, "You are going to hell," and other garbage not worth mentioning. I turned around and started laughing as I recognized this powerless liar, who showed me all of his cards as I walked away.

The apostle John wrote in one of his last letters to his spiritual kids, "Beloved, do not believe every spirit, but test the spirits, whether they are of God."[2] Spirits talk to us, which is why John said to test them and don't believe every voice you hear. If that voice has a tone that wouldn't SPEAK the way a loving father would SPEAK to his kids, it can be flushed and thrown away[2a].

Jesus said that the devil is a liar, and the father of all lies. He seeks to kill, steal, and destroy by SPEAKING lies that sound mostly true, and he usually SPEAKS in a situation where fear is present. Reinhard Bonnke said, "The devil is a mouse with a microphone!" That is the best description of his voice I have ever heard.

When there has been a traumatic situation in our past, or a painful moment where we didn't understand why things happened the way they did, the enemy of our souls comes like a bully and attempts to sow weeds in the garden of our thoughts to get us to believe the lie that God simply checked out in our hard time.

For example, say your parents go through a divorce. In the midst of the pain and confusion the enemy will SPEAK things like, "If you were worth fighting for, your dad wouldn't have left," or, "If God cared for you, then this wouldn't have happened." What you believe forms the lens through which you view the world. If you believe these lies, then the next time you face something even remotely painful, that lens will reappear, and the fear will tell you it's happening again. It will confirm the lie that you are unprotected, alone, and have to fend for yourself—that God is only with you when there is nothing painful going on.

As we talked about in chapter 4, these are strongholds in our minds that we must tear down, and replace with the

[2] 1 John 4:1
[2a] John 10:3-5

stronghold of the Lord, which is built through an agreement with truth. We have to go back to the painful memories and ask our friend the Holy Spirit where Jesus was in those painful memories. He will be faithful to show us where He was every time and reestablish His faithful voice in our lives. God always SPEAKS.

[GOD SPEAKS MORE THAN ENGLISH]

Communication is a lot more than words. In my family, we can communicate through a smile, laughter, or a scowl, because we know each other. My wife can look at me a certain way and I could write a whole book on what she just said to me. Even my chocolate lab Rocky looks at me when it's time to eat with that adorable face like he's saying, "Now? Are we eating now?"

God's voice cannot be limited to one language. He was God before English was invented, and has always been SPEAKING to people. We have been created with five senses and God can SPEAK to us through them all—touch, taste, smell, hearing, and sight. We have also been given an imagination, which is a gift from God. Like anything, when it gets polluted by the world, it becomes destructive. But a sanctified imagination is powerful, because it enables us to see and imagine what God wants to do. Our imagination is like a TV screen for Holy Spirit to SPEAK through.

God SPEAKS to us as a father SPEAKS to sons and daughters. I understand this more today as the father of two kids. One day, I was in my house in Salt Lake City when I heard the Lord say to me about my newborn son, "He is going to change your life more than you are going to change his." This baffled me, because I knew as his father I would be the one raising him. But I tucked it away in my heart. Then I began to have life-changing encounters with God as I was fathering my own son. The love I felt for him was so powerful in me that it led me to SPEAK a life of love and affirmation over him that brought me great joy! It was in these moments where the Holy Spirit would remind me that what I was feeling for my son was a fraction of what He feels for me.

I began to discover that the reason I used to struggle with the voice of God so much was because I didn't understand who I was in my identity. I am His son, and He is my Father! And this is the context of the relationship with God in which I get to experience Him.

I correct my kids to protect them and call them to their potential. I don't shame them in their "dirt"—I call out the gold in them and remind them of who they are. If I need to correct an attitude or behavior, I remind them in a loving way that their behavior or attitude doesn't reflect who they are, and give them grace to change in a shame-free environment. My grace empowers them to rise to my beliefs about them. As an imperfect father, I have messed up many times and had to repent to my kids for being too sharp in a moment, but God never messes up. His tone is always gracious, loving and kind. However, He can be firm and is still the Lord.

[GOD SPEAKS THROUGH THE STILL, SMALL VOICE]

Elijah was a powerful prophet the Lord used to confront idolatry and evil people in the nation of Israel. At one point, he got scared and ran for his life from a crazy witch-queen named Jezebel. As powerful as Elijah was, he was struggling, believing he was alone. Then God told him:

> "Go out, and stand on the mountain before the Lord." And behold, the Lord passed by, and a

great and strong wind tore into the mountains and broke the rocks in pieces before the Lord, but the Lord was not in the wind; and after the wind an earthquake, but the Lord was not in the earthquake; and after the earthquake a fire, but the Lord was not in the fire; and after the fire a still small voice.[3]

Then the Lord told Elijah what to do next, but also let him know he was not alone. In fact, there were seven thousand people still standing for the Lord. This story shows us when we are fearful, God is gentle and SPEAKS to us in the still, small voice to our hearts and minds.

[GOD SPEAKS THROUGH THE WORD OF GOD]

God will never SPEAK something that contradicts His written Word. In fact, He said through the psalmist, "You have magnified Your word above all Your name."[4] When we read His written Word, we will begin to hear His spoken word.

King David said, "Your word I have hidden in my heart, that I might not sin against You."[5]

I have a long history of connection with my kids. Sometimes they will come ask me a question and when they walk away with their answer I will hear them say, "I knew you were going to say that." When we develop a history in God's Word, our ears begin to tune into what He will say to us. Sometimes I can't hear what He's saying, so I just read what He has said in His Word till I hear what He is saying. God always SPEAKS.

[3] 1 Kings 19:11-12
[4] Psalm 138:2
[5] Psalm 119:11

[GOD SPEAKS THROUGH OTHERS]

In 2011, the Lord spoke to me through Shawn Bolz at a conference at Bethel Church. He said:

> Tom and Leslie. I saw you... you're the youth pastors, no? Yeah? I saw you like, erecting something here... I saw towers. I saw two towers, and I felt like September eleventh might be significant to you—that make sense?

I responded, "My birthday and wedding anniversary."

Shawn continued:

> That's your birthday and the day you got married!
>
> Gods acknowledging this day, because He is acknowledging your life. Because He has so pre-planned it. You've got such a strong destiny. You have the power to not only bring a movement for the youth, but actual sustainable resources to keep it going from generation to generation. And you're not just in a position for like a year; you're in a position that God defined for you, [that] He's created you for. That's why I saw your birthday—He created you for this position, for this season. And you're going to erect something, even if it is a birthday or anniversary. It is also two movements you're going to help birth through here, and it reminded me very much of how Banning did Jesus Culture and the youth movement at the same time. You're going to do something that affects the outside and the inside, and the Lord's going to raise you up as a voice.

I was so encouraged by this word. I felt so believed in by God and everyone else there!

Some of the greatest strength I've received is from God SPEAKING through others. The Bible calls this prophecy. Prophetic words will bring edification, strength, and comfort.

I've heard well-meaning believers say, "I don't need anyone else but God." Though I hear what they are trying to say, the truth is that God designed us to need each other in a healthy way. We are called the body of Christ. The foot needs the arm, the toe needs the foot, and the head needs the neck, etc.

Years ago, I began to pursue spiritual mothers and fathers to SPEAK into my life, and it has brought me strength and grace I did not earn. God is the one who raises up leaders, parents, teachers, and coaches, through whom He leads us. People are imperfect, but the Holy Spirit SPEAKS through imperfect people all the time. We can't get religious and turn off the voice of God because we don't like who it's coming through. Have you ever had a friend or parent say, "You've changed since dating that person, or hanging out with those friends." Sometimes, if our hearts are not in a place to hear things from the Lord, He uses others to get our attention.

If I am SPEAKING to a crowd of five hundred people, there are five hundred different messages being heard because the Holy Spirit will SPEAK to each of us what He wants to say in the moment. This is why the Bible tells us, "Do not forsake the gathering together of yourselves."[6] God SPEAKS in the corporate gathering in ways we can't hear in any other way. This should inspire us to make going to youth group or church services a priority! We get to hear from God together!

---

[6] Hebrews 10:25

[GOD SPEAKS THROUGH CREATION]

The psalmist declared, "The heavens proclaim the glory of God. The skies display his craftsmanship."[7] From the ocean to the mountains, or a newborn baby to the solar system, all of creation declares the glory of God! The Holy Spirit loves to SPEAK through His handiwork. I am fascinated by creation! When I see a huge whale jumping out of the water, it feels crazy to think that the same God who made that, loves me. He made it all for us to be enjoyed.

If you follow heaven's design, there is no confusion about many issues that man is trying to recreate. The vast ocean declares the depth of His love, and the mountains declare His majesty. The universe declares the awesomeness of God, and the seasons declare His ways. Mankind declares who He is, for we were made in His image, and we are the apex of all of His creation.

[GOD SPEAKS THROUGH VISIONS AND DREAMS]

Years ago, I had a dream in the middle of the night. It was like a movie I had watched. I was in a dark alley with two kids on one side of the street and one kid on the other side. They were calling each other on like they were about to fight. I could tell the one kid who was by himself was terrified, but the only way he knew how to defend himself was by trying to act tougher than the other kids. All of a sudden, the two kids started chasing the one kid down the alleyway and a bunch of other kids appeared to join in as they began beating him up. All I could do was stand there and watch. I was shaken as he was screaming for his life, taking the beatings from the other boys.

---

[7] Psalm 19:1 NLT

When I came out of the dream, I felt like God was trying to show me something but I couldn't see it. So, I approached one of my friends, who has been interpreting dreams for years, and told him the dream. He immediately saw what God was trying to show me. The Lord was saying to me that as a father, it was time for me to equip kids to disarm the enemy by learning to come in the opposite spirit—to confront the spirit of fear with the spirit of love. God was giving me a strategy to teach a generation how to partner with what God was doing in a situation, rather than react to what the enemy was doing, which got this kid beat up.

Scripture is full of instances in which God spoke through dreams and visions. Jesus' life was saved because God warned Jesus' father, Joseph, about Herod's plot to murder Him. God gave Peter a vision that led to the gospel breaking out of the Jewish world and being preached to everyone. Dreams and visions are the language of the Spirit through which God SPEAKS.

THE WORLD IS WAITING TO HEAR YOUR REDEMPTION

——————— *story.*

OWN IT. LOVE IT. LIVE IT.

TOM CRANDALL

CHAPTER [6]

LET YOUR LIFE SPEAK, PART 1

My wife Leslie grew up in the rolling hills of Pennsylvania in a good home with a mom and dad who loved God and each other. One Sunday when she was five years old, she received a little craft in Sunday School with a lamb on it that said, "Jesus loves ewe." As the family drove home from their Methodist church, Leslie asked her mom, "Is it true if I ask Jesus in my heart, I will go to heaven?"

Her mom said, "Yes, you just ask Jesus into your heart."

At that moment in the car, Leslie asked the Lord to come into her life. He did, and He never left. Never once did Leslie walk away from God or give into the pressure of the world, because nothing the world had to offer was better than her relationship with God. She used to climb a tree near her house to dream and talk with the Lord. Conversing with God became her normal. At fifteen, she got baptized in the Holy Spirit and was powerfully connected to the river of God.

Proud of her story, she never gave into feeling like she had an inferior testimony to someone who was delivered from drugs, sexual immorality, or worldly living. She simply loved God, and it wasn't cool to live any other way. She was raised in innocence, a quality from heaven the world needs.

Choosing a lifestyle apart from God's best just never made sense to her.

She had an amazing friend group that genuinely loved each other and experienced God and life together. They considered gossip and back-stabbing abnormal and didn't tolerate it. They thought it would be gross to act like that.

During Leslie's senior year in high school, she and a couple of her friends wanted to see God move, so they started praying on their campus, believing God for revival. God began to pour out His Spirit in such a powerful, real way that people began to come before school in order to pray. Upon graduation, Leslie left to attend ministry school, and her group of friends with whom she had started the group continued to meet weekly to pray. Eventually, over a thousand young people were coming together to seek God every week! It was a revival that began to reach thousands of people in their community and lasted for years. This move of God started with a group of friends who owned their story, were unashamed of Jesus, and let their lives SPEAK!

[OWN YOUR STORY]

I have met hundreds of Christians who feel like they don't have a powerful testimony because they didn't get saved out of an immoral, sin-filled life. They don't feel empowered to share their story because the lies they believed told them they didn't have one to share. How about this for a story—"God is good and His friendship is so powerful that there is nothing good for me outside of God! He saved me from a life of sin that I never had to live, protected me from unnecessary pain and heartache, preserved me and empowered me to live a supernatural life like Jesus!" Sounds pretty good to me. If this is your story, then be like my wife—own it!

Or maybe your story sounds more like mine or others who needed massive forgiveness. (Of course, the truth is that we all need forgiveness.) Over the years, I've seen many people share stories about how they've been on drugs and slept around, and then got saved. Then they drop the mic and walk away. I want to say, "Hey, whoa. Hold on here. Telling the world about all the bad things you did is only a part of your story, and it does help break shame. But declaring what Jesus has done in your life is where the power comes from for you and others to move forward in grace." It really is all about Jesus, not our junk.

[LET YOUR LIFE SPEAK: REDEMPTION'S STORY]

As an eight-year-old boy, Ken was a smaller-framed kid, and was often called "shrimp" and "faggot." He grew to believe that masculinity was inappropriate and unspiritual, and had difficulty receiving affection from his dad and other males. After being exposed to homosexual porn at ten, he felt shameful and damaged with nowhere to turn. Eventually his inner thought-life consistently told him that he must be gay. In desperation, he went to the Christian bookstore looking for help and couldn't find a single resource that offered any hope.

After battling same-sex attraction for over ten years and having little hope that he could ever get free, God supernaturally healed Ken of a severe acid reflux disorder. He thought, *If God can heal me of that, surely He can heal my broken sexuality.* So, he began to pursue God in every revival meeting he could find and read every book about the power of God he could get his hands on. He began to meet regularly with a father figure who unconditionally loved him, yet gave him honest feedback that helped him find hope and experience transformation.

The healing of his sexual identity was a process for Ken that included belonging to a Spirit-led community, practicing vulnerability, spending time in the presence of God, replacing lies with God's truth, and receiving healing of emotional pain and wounding. Over time, God healed Ken profoundly. He is now married to a beautiful lady, has four children, and has been a pastor on staff at Bethel Church since 2006. He stands on large stages around the world, giving hope to people confused about their sexual identity so that they can be healed by the unconditional love and power of God! Ken has also partnered with his other once-gay friends and launched a ministry called Equipped to Love, which teaches the church how to effectively love those who are impacted by homosexuality. The redemption for Ken is that he now gets to offer consulting to those who are battling homosexuality—the very thing that was his greatest weakness.[1]

No one is beyond redemption. No matter what you're in the middle of now, your life can speak of an overcoming story of redemption like millions of others throughout history. Jesus took the sin of the world on Himself on the cross, providing the only way to the Father through Him. Trusting Jesus with your life is the only path to redemption. He is the only way to God!

Good works and being religious will never redeem us or make things right. Only Jesus dying in our place was enough to bring redemption and freedom. The apostle Paul said, "Therefore, if anyone is in Christ, he is a new creation. The old has passed away; behold, the new has come."[2]

You can't add to the blood of Jesus. As a young believer, I killed feelings of unworthiness by declaring, "If I can

---

[1] You can visit Ken's website to learn more about his ministry: KenWilliamsMinistries.com

[2] 2 Corinthians 5:17 ESV

earn redemption, then Christ died in vain!" No one is good enough to earn redemption; it's a gift from God and must be received as such!

Years ago, I was speaking at juvenile hall in Redding. I illustrated this point by holding up a Bible. I began to tear out all the books that were written by redeemed people who had murdered someone in their past. The first five books of the Bible, written by Moses, were the first to go. Next, I tore out the Psalms, most of which were written by King David. Then I tore out the thirteen books in the New Testament written by the apostle Paul, who used to murder Christians!

The eyes of the young people in my audience were as big as saucers as they looked at the sacred pages of the Bible lying on the ground. Then I said, "We rip our own lives out of redemption's story and are more offended at this paper on the ground than we are that our lives are not in His story. Moses murdered an Egyptian, Noah got drunk, Abraham lied, King David committed adultery then murdered someone attempting to cover it up, Peter denied Christ when He needed him the most, and the apostle Paul murdered Christians before getting saved! Moses delivered Israel, Noah preserved the human race, Abraham is the father of faith, King David was known as a man after God's own heart. Peter was crucified upside down for Christ, and Paul the apostle influenced the world for Christ!"

Shame was stripped away as the unconditional love of God filled the hall. The roadblocks to Jesus were removed by the testimonies of His grace on imperfect heroes of the past. Faith was born, and kids' hearts were mended as they responded to His love.

God is a redeemer, who will give:

> ...beauty for ashes,

The oil of joy for mourning,

The garment of praise for the spirit of heaviness;

That they may be called trees of righteousness,

The planting of the LORD, that He may be glorified."[3]

Redemption doesn't happen in a liturgical monastery, but in a relational family. Knowing you're forgiven by God empowers you to forgive yourself and others and shapes you into an overcomer. Maybe your story doesn't feel great right now, but the book of your life isn't finished. If you will follow Jesus and never quit, God will write a story with anyone's life that will SPEAK a message of hope the world needs to hear!

[LET YOUR LIFE SPEAK SONSHIP]

The words of Jesus created life. He spoke from the heart of His Father and imparted a new operating system to all who received them. The operating system of life that Jesus imparted was *sonship*. He was not just "the Son of God." He was a great Son who was connected to His Father, which was why His life spoke only of what the Father was doing. God the Father sent Jesus the Son to an orphaned planet to invite us into a family relationship. The apostle John said that when we received Him, He gave us the right to become children of God.[4] Paul said, "For you did not receive the spirit of bondage again to fear, but you received the Spirit of adoption by whom we cry out, 'Abba, Father.'"[5] "Abba" means "Daddy" God. This term of affection gives such a powerful description of what our relationship can SPEAK.

When our perception of God the Father is that He is close, caring, gentle, loving, and kind, our lives will SPEAK the

---

[3] Isaiah 61:3

[4] John 1:12

[5] Romans 8:15

same message. Jesus told us to approach God and call Him "Our Father in heaven."

If you ever meet my kids, you'll notice that they sound a lot like me and their mom. It is the same in letting your life SPEAK as a son or daughter of God. As we abide in His love and He abides in us, we will sound like our Father!

I've meet hundreds of people who cringe when you mention the word "Father" or "family" because of the negative experience they've had, but God is good regardless of our experience. He has gracious and open arms to heal all who come to Him, so they can have a new, safe, and awesome experience with the Father.

One of my spiritual daughters battled feelings of unworthiness and abandonment because her father moved away years ago and has hardly maintained any connection with her. One day, she encountered the Father. She came out of that encounter beaming, and told me, "Tom, God told me I've never been fatherless. It's a lie. He has always fathered me!" The Holy Spirit took her back to the painful times where she felt alone and showed her how He was there for her in the hardest times of her life. Her life SPEAKS a redemption story, and still SPEAKS hope today.

[YOU'VE CONQUERED SHAME]

The Bible describes the devil as a thief, liar, and a murderer. The enemy uses the feeling of shame to rob you in all three ways. Conviction is what you feel when you do something wrong, which can lead you to clean up messes you've made. Shame, on the other hand, is the feeling that there is something wrong with you, and leaves you feeling hopeless about your life. Nothing will rob your life and story more than shame. The voice of shame says:

"*Shh.* Don't let anyone know your story—they won't accept you."

"You're not good enough to know God."

"God could never speak through you. You've done too much."

These are all lies of shame. The voice of shame attempts to muffle the voice of God's people, crippling them from letting their lives SPEAK the message the world so desperately needs to hear.

We don't defeat shame in our story by ignoring it, but by running at it. John the apostle, who walked with Jesus, said, "But if we walk in the light as He is in the light, we have fellowship with one another, and the blood of Jesus Christ His Son cleanses us from all sin."[6] Ken ran towards healing until he was free. You beat the voice of shame by exposing it in the light to the Lord and others. Who is someone trustworthy you can talk to about the shame that's shutting down your story?

[LET YOUR LIFE SPEAK: COURAGE]

On September 11, 2001, the world witnessed one of the most courageous acts in history. After two jumbo jets hit the Twin Towers in New York City, 343 of the world's bravest firefighters poured into the World Trade Center to rescue hundreds of people from the burning buildings before losing their lives. Something can be learned from these courageous men. In the face of the worst possible circumstances a man could face, they went anyways. They didn't let the circumstances define them on that horrific day. They let their courage SPEAK for the whole world to see.

---

[6] 1 John 1:7

We watch movies and think that courage looks like Tony Stark or Captain America, but unless you have a billion-dollar suit or superpowers, that's not real. Courage looks like Desmond Doss from *Hacksaw Ridge*, William Wallace from *Braveheart,* or Rosa Parks, who stood up with all the odds stacked against her.

If you ever get the chance to lay down your life for another, you probably won't feel courageous. You will feel fear. Yet, to quote Mark Twain once more: "Courage is not the lack of fear. It's acting in spite of it." I have faced my own fears many times and walked away with the satisfaction of knowing I beat fear again and allowed my courage to define me.

Courage in everyday life looks different than running into a burning building. Brené Brown says, "Courage starts with showing up and letting ourselves be seen."[7] It looks like being vulnerable enough to let others see you and see where you need help. I have met some of the bravest teenagers in the world who have used these words, "I have been struggling with porn," "I am afraid," or "I don't know what to do." Many times, this is what courage sounds like.

How is the Holy Spirit leading you to be courageous today? Courage is the first step towards owning your story and letting your life SPEAK. You don't have to let fear and shame rob you anymore. You can let your life SPEAK courage louder than your fears.

---

[7] Brené Brown, *Daring Greatly: How the Courage to Be Vulnerable Transforms the Way We Live, Parent, and Lead* (New York: Penguin Publishing Group, 2012), 30.

speech
life
love
faith
purity

[1 TIMOTHY 4:12]

CHAPTER [7]

LET YOUR LIFE SPEAK, PART 2

A lot of people in the world SPEAK, but have nothing to say. When our words either don't match our life, or we don't SPEAK truth, what we say doesn't go anywhere. Jesus said, "The words that I speak to you are spirit, and they are life."[1]

As you read in chapter 2, Mari's life began to SPEAK so loud that everyone wanted to hear what she had to say. She got alone with God, developed a relationship with the Holy Spirit, and began to carry the presence of God, which SPEAKS louder than words. The daily choices she made set an example for everyone else to follow.

[BE AN EXAMPLE]

The apostle Paul wrote a letter to his spiritual son, Timothy, on how to let his life SPEAK. Paul said, "Don't let anyone look down on you because you are young, but set an example for the believers in speech, in life, in love, in faith and in purity."[2]

Everything in the New Testament needs to be seen through the lenses of Jesus, who modeled a life yielded to

---

[1] John 6:63
[2] 1 Timothy 4:12 NIV

His Father. Jesus set an example for us by doing only what He saw His Father doing, through the Holy Spirit. He showed us that being an example can't be watered down to sheer morality or not doing any number of bad things. Being an example means bringing the gospel of the kingdom everywhere we go! Following Christ is not about a list of dos and don'ts, but about being empowered by His grace to live like He did on the earth.

Jesus lived and preached the gospel, or good news, of the kingdom. Again, *kingdom* means a sphere of influence where the King reigns. Jesus taught us to pray: "Your kingdom come. Your will be done on earth as it is in heaven."[3] When we follow the Holy Spirit, our lives will start looking like the example Jesus set. We will bring love, healing, and power to those around us. The kingdom of God is in the presence of God, which is why understanding what you carry as a believer is essential to partnering with God to release heaven on earth! We carry His presence with the authority of the King. Letting our lives SPEAK cannot be reduced to using words alone, but releasing the kingdom of God in power and love.

The reason you don't need to "let anyone look down on you because you are young," is because there is no junior Holy Spirit. You don't get a "Happy Meal" Jesus, while the adults get the "Super-Size Me" Jesus. Believing you are inferior as a young person is empowering the lie that you have nothing to give, and your faith will be hindered as a result.

Setting an example starts with having a heart that seeks to honor God and follow Jesus in the simple, mundane things of life. It might start with making your bed, how you treat your family and friends, and what you entertain on your iPhone and social media pages.

---

[3] Matthew 6:10

If you want to preach and no one is asking you to, don't ask for a place to preach. Rather, seek to serve and let your life SPEAK, and eventually someone will want to hear what you have to say. Think about your favorite movie or You-Tubers, and I'll bet some of them are setting an inspiring example. What if your life inspired everyone around you to follow the example Jesus showed us?

[LET YOUR LIFE SPEAK IN SPEECH]

Our mouth is a portal for heaven or hell. The attitudes of our hearts will determine which source we SPEAK from. When Jesus told His disciples He was going to go to the cross, Peter rebuked him. Jesus told him, "Get behind Me, Satan! You are an offense to Me, for you are not mindful of the things of God, but the things of men."[4] Ouch! Jesus equated the "things of man" as Satanic when they work against God's will.

Gossip is partnering with the devil's lies and destruction over another person, which releases division and strife in friendships. Cursing ourselves with words releases a demonic spirit of self-hatred, causing us to see ourselves inaccurately.

The Holy Spirit has been a faithful friend to convict me of my words and help me stay true to who I am with what I SPEAK about myself and others. I have often found myself repenting for saying something that didn't reflect who I was.

Jesus used words many times to heal, encourage, and release the kingdom of God to people. Paul told the church in Corinth, "Pursue love, and desire spiritual gifts, but especially that you may prophesy."[5] To *prophesy* means to de-

---

[4] Matthew 16:23
[5] 1 Corinthians 14:1

clare what God sees. God is a good Father who, like a gold miner, calls out the gold in everyone. I've never heard of a gold miner saying, "Wow, look at that dirt! It's hopeless. Let's just go home." A gold miner sees the gold and mines it out. God is the same way when He looks at our lives. The way He SPEAKS to us brings the gold to the surface.

As I mentioned before, when my kids have done something wrong or struggled, I don't shame them; I remind them of who they are and how I see them. It's the same in the kingdom. What if we set an example by declaring over each other what we heard the Father saying? It would change the game!

The Lord brought a man named Ezekiel into an encounter in which He showed him a valley of dry bones. He then told Ezekiel to prophesy, saying:

> "'Dry bones, hear the word of the Lord! This is what the Sovereign Lord says to these bones: I will make breath enter you, and you will come to life. I will attach tendons to you and make flesh come upon you and cover you with skin; I will put breath in you, and you will come to life. Then you will know that I am the Lord.'"
>
> So I prophesied as I was commanded. And as I was prophesying, there was a noise, a rattling sound, and the bones came together, bone to bone... Then he said to me, "Prophesy to the breath; prophesy, son of man, and say to it, 'This is what the Sovereign Lord says: Come from the four winds, O breath, and breathe into these slain, that they may live.'" So I prophesied as He commanded me, and breath entered them; they came to life and stood up on their feet—a vast army.[6]

---

[6] Ezekiel 37:4-10

What if Ezekiel said to God, "Sorry, no. The bones are too dry. It just won't work. Not feeling it today."

One girl, who had never been to church before and didn't know anything about Jesus, came to Young Saints. Another teenager, who had learned to prophesy, approached her during worship and gave her a prophetic word. It awakened her heart, and she gave her life to Christ right there.

We can use our words to SPEAK life and see dry bones come together, no matter how dry things may seem, and be a part of seeing a vast army of the redeemed arise. We can set an example for other believers in how we SPEAK!

[LET YOUR LIFE SPEAK IN LIFE]

As the saying goes, actions speak louder than words. When we back up declaring the gospel with action, we make it believable to others. On the other hand, when we don't live what we say, we rob our words of power. God wants our lives to SPEAK in agreement with our words.

Mari faithfully led worship for Young Saints as a volunteer for over eleven years before we hired her. As I mentioned in chapter 2, before coming on staff as our worship leader, Mari worked as a dental assistant. What I didn't say was that before hiring Mari, the dentist who owned the practice had been leery of people who said they went to Bethel Church because of getting burned by previous patients and employees who claimed to follow Christ, yet didn't pay their bills or were just irresponsible in their example.

When Mari started working, her boss and fellow employees knew she attended Bethel and didn't know what to expect from her—until they saw the example she set with the life she lived. Seeing Mari show up early, leave late, and work hard made her boss feel like such a genius for hiring her that his perspective of Bethel changed. Because Mari let her life SPEAK, it drowned out the bad impressions of the past and helped his heart open up to the things of God. The dentist began to get hungry for God, which led to some incredible encounters and miracles in the office that brought him and his family into personal revival!

One day, the dentist's son was hit with a dodgeball on his bare eyeball. The urgent care doctor they visited said the boy's eyeball was swelling, and that there could be a scratch on it. The dentist pulled Mari aside and asked her to pray for his son. After she prayed, the swelling got visibly better, but not 100 percent. By the time they got to the eye doctor, however, the dentist's son was feeling almost completely better. The eye doctor said there was not even a micro-scratch and that his eye was totally fine. Today, the dentist and his family attend Bethel Church.

Setting an example through our lives can range from how we treat the substitute teacher to showing up on time to a job or team practice. There is something so fulfilling about owning your own life and being responsible with the little things in life. We let our lives SPEAK through the life we live!

[LET YOUR LIFE SPEAK IN LOVE]

At twenty-two, I had a job driving a concrete truck. My boss was a Vietnam veteran named Chuck, an angry guy who cussed me out at the drop of a hat in front of my coworkers. He made my life very difficult as his employee. I tried to kill his flame of anger with my water of kindness, but it didn't seem to go anywhere. When I told him I was getting married, he belittled me, making me feel so stupid. It didn't take long to discover that he was a very hurting individual who took it out on everyone he was leading at the concrete plant.

The Holy Spirit whispered in my heart to keep loving Chuck and killing him with kindness, so I began to take his tirades as an opportunity to pray for him and show him what love looks like. It wasn't easy between the cuss words, but I continued to pray for him, be a good employee, and be as kind as I could. After months of this, one day we ended up in the dispatch room alone, and he began to open up about painful things in his life. I listened and told him that God loves him. He snapped back, "Do you think so?" Amazingly, he let me pray for him. Everything changed that day. Chuck softened, and it actually became fun to work for him.

Nothing is more powerful than the love of God! The Bible uses the Greek word *agape* to describe the love of God. *Agape* means perfect, unconditional love—love that never changes, that totally accepts and delights in others, and that always gives generously and sacrificially for others' good. God loves because that's who He is. In order to demonstrate His love to others, we must first receive it for ourselves. Ken Williams says, "You can't receive unconditional love unless you show your condition." No matter your condition, God will never reject you. You can show Him everything and He will still love you!

In our worst moments, God's love never changes, which sets Him apart from every other love in the world. When people show us their worst, that is the time to show them our best. If we refuse to put on the blindfold of offense, we will see to love them for who they really are and bring out the best in them through the power of consistent love. Imagine a hose connected to the top of your head and the bottom of your feet with love coming in and going out. We can become a conduit of the love of God.

We don't love people to get them saved; we love them because God loves them, and they will want God as a result. Scripture says, "The only thing that counts is faith expressing itself through love."[7] *Agape* demonstrates the same love that drove Jesus to the cross for all of humanity. Love always moves in the opposite spirit of this world. When people show us anger, love SPEAKS gentleness. When they show rudeness, love SPEAKS patience and kindness. When others are selfish, love SPEAKS giving. When others gossip, love SPEAKS protection. When others give up, love SPEAKS hope.

The Holy Spirit describes love through the apostle Paul better than any piece of literature in the history of the world:

> If I speak in the tongues of men and of angels, but have not love, I am only a resounding gong or a clanging cymbal. If I have the gift of prophecy and can fathom all mysteries and all knowledge, and if I have a faith that can move mountains, but have not love, I am nothing. If I give all I possess to the poor and surrender my body to the flames, but have not love, I gain nothing.
>
> Love is patient, love is kind. It does not envy, it does not boast, it is not proud. It is not rude, it is not self-seeking, it is not easily angered, it keeps no record of wrongs. Love does not delight in evil but rejoices with the truth. It always protects, always trusts, always hopes, always perseveres. Love never fails.[8]

Love is better experienced than explained. If we stay open to the Lord and let Him love us through every season, His

---

[7] Galatians 5:6 NIV

[8] 1 Corinthians 1:1-18

agape love will SPEAK through us in ways that will conquer hearts around us.

[LET YOUR LIFE SPEAK IN FAITH]

Jacob was excited to come with us to Mexico on a mission trip. He had never seen a miracle, but he wanted to see God move in miraculous ways like he had heard about.

On one of the final nights, we were given a short time to preach and pray for people, so I gave a really fast explanation of Jesus and the kingdom of God, then released our students to pray for people in the crowd.

Jacob and another student began praying for a man who had a tumor on his back the size of a baseball. Jacob suddenly felt heat come on him like he was on fire, then put his hand on the tumor and yelled, "Tumor be gone!" Jacob felt the tumor shrink under his hand until it was totally gone. The healed man started yelling at the top of his lungs that God had healed him.

Jacob was still freaking out about the miracle he had witnessed as we got on the bus to leave. It was so fun to hear Jacob describe what had just happened!

Scripture says, "But without faith it is impossible to please Him, for he who comes to God must believe that He is, and that He is a rewarder of those who diligently seek Him."[9] Faith in Jesus is simple. It's trusting that He is who He says He is, that you are who He says you are, and that He will do what He says He will do. Faith can be defined as simple trust that leads to an action, which results in His world breaking into this one. Faith is the currency of the kingdom. It allows His reality to come into ours. When

---

[9] Hebrews 11:6

this happens, anxiety gets swallowed by peace, fear is confronted by courage, sin drowns in a sea of grace, and sickness bows its knee to the Healer. The weak are made strong and the blind see. Orphans become sons and daughters. We become victorious as we are anchored in the One who never changes, is always good, and paid the price with His own blood for every breakthrough we will ever need.

Faith can look like everything from trusting God for the right friends to praying for someone to be healed from cancer and everything in between. However, faith starts with knowing the will of God, which looks like, "On earth as it is in heaven." Jesus only did what He *saw* His Father doing, which tells us that faith *sees*. The Holy Spirit illuminates to the eyes of our hearts either a problem that we are carrying the solution for, or a solution we are carrying for a problem. We can move with great confidence in the face of impossibilities when we know that what we are believing God for has already been purchased, and He wants it more than we do.

The only way the kingdom of God goes forward in our lives is through faith. Someone has to say "yes" to God! The reason we have the book of Acts is because someone acted in faith, and God moved as a result. Their stories still SPEAK of what the Holy Spirit is doing on the earth.

Setting an example in faith looks like making it a habit to trust God first instead of other options, and walking with God in every area of life. When we trust God with our lives, and put our faith in Jesus regardless of the circumstances, our lives will SPEAK of heaven's solutions for the world to hear.

[LET YOUR LIFE SPEAK IN PURITY]

Purity is beautiful, liberating, and powerful. Like pure water from a fresh geyser, it is uncontaminated and simply good. Purity is the result of encountering triumphant truth and bottomless grace. As we see in the instances where Jesus touched the lepers everyone else ran from, everything Jesus touches becomes pure.

Braden was an athletic and energetic eight-year-old boy who found pornography with a friend at church. Feeling curious about what he saw pulled him into battle with it from that point on. The emotional yo-yo of highs and lows took him from lust to shame and adrenaline to emptiness on a continual basis.

Braden attended our Young Saints Youth Camp in the summer of 2017. One night, our speaker gave a call for anyone to come forward who didn't feel worthy of love. Feeling unlovable because of his addiction, Braden risked it all and went forward. A youth leader came up behind him, hugged him, and said, "You don't need that." Braden felt something dark physically leave his body and he felt instantly lighter. Then the leader said, "I love you." Braden felt the presence of God fill the hole where the dark spirit had left. Braden immediately turned around to say thank you, only to find that no one was there. The youth leader he thought was touching him was the Holy Spirit leading him into freedom and purity. He dropped to his knees and began to weep and worship at the love of God.

Braden was never the same after that encounter. At the next Young Saints youth service, Braden boldly went on stage and told everyone how God had set him free from years of porn, guilt, and shame. His testimony gave so much hope to struggling kids that a bunch more responded to get free in the moment.

Today, you can see the freedom in Braden's eyes and purity that came as a result of surrendering to a love encounter with God. Braden's life SPEAKS purity and freedom.

If you need this freedom, take courage from Braden's story and receive it!

[LET YOUR LIFE SPEAK IN YOUR GIFTS AND PASSIONS]

From the age of eight, British-born Joshy Altamura not only had a passion to cook—he was actually very good at it. Instead of following recipes, he learned to create organically by taste. After realizing at twelve years old that he came alive by creating delicious pieces of art that satisfied others, he began to pursue his dreams of becoming a chef.

One day, Joshy was watching the hit Netflix show *Chopped* when the host, Ted Allen, mentioned their kids show, *Chopped Junior*. Joshy went straight to YouTube and began to watch all the content available from the show. As he watched other kids living out his dream, he said, "I can do that. What if I signed up?"

So Joshy did. After filling out the application form and submitting a signature dish proposal—steak, potato croquettes, and asparagus—the audition process began. It was grueling and lasted around three months. After myriad phone and FaceTime calls later, along with two documentaries charting him cooking, Joshy was chosen to be a contestant on *Chopped Junior*!

Joshy flew to New York City and competed for a week with America's top junior chefs. At the end of the week, Joshy was crowned the winner on the show, and was asked to be a judge on the next episode: "Make Me A Judge!" This episode was the first of its kind for the Food Network. Joshy had the honor of judging three of America's top chefs—and "Chopping" them.

Joshy was sworn to secrecy about these results until the show aired. Bethel hosted a viewing of the show on the church campus, and many people from the church and Young Saints showed up to watch. Everyone was so proud of Joshy! His kindness and honor towards the other contestants was evident on the show. It was also obvious that he had truly created the most creative and tasty dishes of all the junior chefs.

But Joshy's story doesn't end there. Sometime after winning the show, we announced at our Young Saints weekly youth service that we would be giving to a mission project to support a missionary named Tracy Evans, who works in in Mozambique. She needed $10,000 to build a school. She had already built a similar school in another village where an Islamic mosque was being built, and through the influence of the school, the entire village had come to Christ and the mosque had not been used once.

When Josh he heard this vision, he felt moved in his heart to give $1,000 of his winnings from *Chopped Junior* to the mission project.

The psalmist David said, "Delight yourself in the Lord and he will give you the desires of your heart."[10] Many young people feel like they have to choose between God or their favorite sport, or between God and something they are good at. But unless the desire of your heart is sinful or you're loving it more than God, it's not in conflict with love for God. The Father actually gives us the desires of our hearts, then leads us to become excellent at them, which enables us to demonstrate His goodness to the world.

---

[10] Psalm 37:4

Joshy loves cooking, and through it he puts kindness, excellence, creativity, and generosity on display. Recently, he got to cook and create food for kids on a mission trip to Mexico and show that God loves them. He lets his life SPEAK boldly through his passion for cooking. What do you love? When you dedicate your passions to the Lord and you've owned your redemption story, your passions become a platform for your life to SPEAK!

Historically, the church has created a divide between the "secular" and the "sacred" and applied this in ways God never did. This divide treats things like preaching behind a pulpit or leading worship as sacred and therefore approved by God (and they are), but things like fishing or dance as secular and therefore not holy and spiritual. However, God has erased these lines, and so should we. The apostle Paul said, "Work willingly at whatever you do, as though you were working for the Lord rather than for people."[11] When your heart burns with a passion to honor God and lift Jesus up, do whatever you find yourself doing with all of your might and you can glorify God through what you love! Put in the work to become the best you can be at basketball, art, tennis, acting, or whatever your passion and gift might be. When you work hard to develop your gift and do it as unto the Lord and not for men, God anoints anything you do because you are the one carrying the anointing. Jesus will be exalted through what your life SPEAKS for the whole world to hear!

---

[11] Colossians 3:23 NLT

"

EMBRACING YOUR MOMENT EMPOWERS OTHERS TO STEP INTO THEIRS.

IT'S YOUR TIME TO SHINE!

"

TOM CRANDALL

CHAPTER [8]

NOW IS THE TIME TO LET YOUR LIFE SPEAK

A round five years ago, our youth ministry supported a Bethel missionary on a couple of projects. This brave young woman, whom we will call Amanda, knew that it was time for her life to SPEAK. After graduating from the Bethel School of Supernatural Ministry, she responded to the call of God to go to South East Asia to reach people who had never heard the good news of Jesus before. She helped lead a small school where kids learned about the love of Christ and His power to save and heal, while seeking refuge from the child army recruiters and sex traffickers.

After spending some time pouring into these kids, Amanda came home for a break. Here is a testimony that took place in Asia while she was at home:

> Two of our students were siblings. The girl was eleven and the boy was thirteen. They were at home in their village on a holiday break after attended our boarding school just across the border. Their father was an alcoholic and was abusive to the family.

> One night, their father got drunk and began fighting with their mother. In tears, she expressed that she no longer wanted to live. The children, being

filled with the Holy Spirit and having discernment, began to pray. That night, their mother woke up, took a bottle of pills, and wandered into the jungle to a quiet place to die. In the morning, the children saw the empty bottle and knew what had happened, so they prayed that God would help them find their mother. They began searching and followed where they felt the Lord was showing them. When they found her, she was lying on the ground. Her body was pale and cold, and they said they knew she had died. They laid their hands on her and began to pray. After about thirty minutes of praying, she suddenly took a deep breath and woke up. The children were so happy and praised God for what He had done! Unfortunately, their mother's first response was anger with her children for bringing her back, but they knew they had just experienced a miracle so they brought her to the school for church on a Sunday morning so that we could help explain to her what happened. Once she understood why she was alive, she gave her life to Christ, and went on to be a powerful voice of protection for the unwanted children in her village.

Amanda recognized her moment, and she courageously went for it. The result is that a group of kids from a Buddhist background found the love of God and raised their mom from the dead, and she now fights for the unwanted. Because Amanda knew it was her time, the kids got to live in their moment to restore their family.

Embracing our moment empowers others to step into theirs!

Could you imagine being on the shores of Galilee when Jesus supernaturally multiplied food to feed over twenty thousand people? Jesus saw a moment from the Father and invited His disciples into it by asking Philip, "Where should we buy bread so they can eat?" The disciples were clueless because they didn't have the money or food to feed them, but Jesus knew what He was doing with His question. He was prodding His disciples to recognize their moment with what was in their hands. Andrew, who was Peter's brother, recognized the moment and found a boy who had five barley loaves and two small fish and brought him to Jesus.

Jesus had the people sit down, gave thanks for the food, and then assigned the disciples to distribute it to those sitting down. There was so much food that afterwards they gathered twelve basketfuls of leftovers![1]

This supernatural story happened because a boy simply offered the little he had to Jesus when it mattered. Most divine opportunities start with us taking the little we have and using it to respond to the need of the moment.

[RECOGNIZING OUR MOMENT]

Jesus was talking to a group of religious leaders called the Pharisees. One of the Pharisees' main obsessions was interpreting the Scriptures, including the prophecies about the promised Messiah. Jesus found Himself in another squabble with them because they couldn't recognize that He was, in fact, the Messiah. He said to them:

> "When evening comes, you say, 'It will be fair weather, for the sky is red,' and in the morning, 'Today it will be stormy, for the sky is red and overcast.' You know how to interpret the

---
[1] Matthew 14:15-21

appearance of the sky, but you cannot interpret the signs of the times."[2]

The Pharisees didn't know what time it was and missed their moment, which was Christ standing right in front of them. Because they didn't believe the miracles they had already seen, they wanted more proof to believe it was their moment.

When Jesus said, "signs of the times," it's important to understand what the word "times" means. In this instance, "times" comes from the Greek word *kairos*, which means time or season. Imagine a car picking up speed in front of you, and you have only moments to jump in the back window. If you are early or late, you'll miss your moment. Or imagine a photographer waiting to capture an image of a majestic animal—there's only a moment to snap the money shot. That is a *kairos* moment.

What is the *kairos* moment standing in front of you today? What is the Holy Spirit leading you towards?

Again, if you are a student on a campus, you are living in one of the largest mission fields in the world. At your junior high or high school campus, you pass by hundreds of people every day. When you graduate and get a job, you will probably work with a lot less people. You can start a club and bring the kingdom of God in power and love right now! Don't miss your moment as a student to reach your campus.

Kairos moments usually start small. In my experience, I'll see a glimpse in my mind of what could be, or sense that if I follow what I'm feeling, whether it be a voice, feeling, or unction, heaven's breakthrough is on the other side.

Recently, I was walking into our mall here in Redding on a rainy day when I noticed a young man standing out front, staring off into the parking lot. I heard a voice in my mind

[2] Matthew 16:2-3 NIV

say, *Go talk to him.* Without giving it too much I thought, I approached him and asked, "Hey man, how are you? I felt like I needed to come talk to you. How's your day going?"

"Doing alright," he replied. "But I'm not very religious."

"Neither am I," I said. *Jesus didn't come to establish a religion, but a relationship!*

Then he said, "What's interesting is that I'm really going through a hard time right now, and I was just standing here kind of praying to myself."

I said, "Wow, think about that! You were standing here praying, God heard your cry, and told me to come talk to you."

Did you see what just happened in this *kairos* moment? Faith was born in this man, making a way for God to enter. He was visibly moved, and so was I. We both knew we were standing in the middle of a divine appointment!

I explained to my friend that God really cares about his life and loves him deeply, and that there is no deeper love to share with the human soul than the story and power of the good news of Jesus Christ! God wants relationship with us. Seeing that sin separated us from Him, He sent His Son Jesus to die on a cross, taking our sin and punishment on Himself to liberate us into a life of connection and power with Him. Jesus received the life we deserved to give us the life He deserved—life everlasting! Then I asked, "Have you ever prayed to invite Christ into your life before?"

"No," he replied.

"Would you like to?"

"Yes, I would."

So right there in front of the mall, with people walking past us, I led this man into a relationship with the Lord.

Then I prayed for him to be baptized in the Holy Spirit. It was a stunning moment as the peace of God came over him. He asked me for a hug and we stood there embracing each other for a long moment. The love of God was so tangible.

It all started with a voice saying, *Go talk to him.* We shared a *kairos* moment that brought heaven to earth in both of our lives.

What *kairos* moment is standing in front of you today? When we obey the voice of the Holy Spirit, our lives will SPEAK what heaven is wanting to say.

[YOU ARE IN YOUR MOMENT FOR SUCH A TIME AS THIS]

About 2,500 years ago, a man named Mordecai helped his cousin, Esther, recognize her moment. Esther was a beautiful woman married to the king of Persia. She was also secretly Jewish. Mordecai, who was also Jewish, heard about a plot to exterminate the Jews led by one of the king's men, Haman. Mordecai sent Esther an urgent message calling her to intervene before the king ordered thousands of innocent people to be slaughtered.

Initially, Esther pushed back on Mordecai, explaining that anyone who entered the king's presence without an invitation would be put to death—including her. Mordecai sent another message in response:

> "Do not think in your heart that you will escape in the king's palace any more than all the other Jews. For if you remain completely silent at this time, relief and deliverance will arise for the Jews from another place, but you and your father's house will

perish. Yet who knows whether you have come to the kingdom for such a time as this?"[3]

After praying and fasting for a few days, Esther bravely entered the king's court without an invitation, knowing that it could mean her death. The king granted her access to his presence, and she was able to tell him of Haman's plot and ask for mercy for her people. In the end, Haman was hanged by the king and the Jews were saved from genocide—all because one brave girl stepped into the moment for which she was born.

Just like Esther, you and I have been brought into the kingdom for such a time as this.

Never before in all of history has this moment happened. You are in the right family, school, city, and friend group for such a time as this to let your life SPEAK.

[LEARN FROM MISTAKES, MOVE FORWARD, AND LET THEM SPEAK]

Years ago, my intern Kyle and I had a brief layover at the Dallas Airport. I looked at my clock and thought that I had enough time to catch a bite to eat on my way to board our connecting flight. Feeling like I should get something healthy, I got a chicken salad (not my lunch of choice), then walked to the gate, which was right across from the restaurant, to board.

Though we still had a few minutes before the flight was about to take off, the flight attendant at the gate said, "I've been looking for you guys. I gave your seats away to a person waiting on standby a few minutes ago, because I didn't think you were coming."

[3] Esther 4:13-14

Shocked and upset, I demanded that he pull those people off the plane and give us our seats. However, it was already too late and he couldn't do it. Kyle and I then learned that we would have to wait twelve hours to catch the next flight home!

We walked away incredibly sad and disappointed, and I threw my salad—the stupid decision that made me late to my flight—into the garbage. As we walked around the terminal, I faced the fact that I hadn't had enough urgency about boarding my flight.

Though I regretted missing my flight, and didn't get to choose my consequences, I eventually decided to laugh at myself and make the best of the day. Kyle and I ended up having a great day walking around the DFW airport. We had some quality time and even ended up leading a guy to the Lord!

Some of us approach the day in which we are living like I approached my connecting flight. I saw my gate, but chose my appetite over being assertive and early, and it cost me dearly. I made a mistake by not observing the time and moving with more urgency. I have since learned from my mistake.

Are you tired of missing your moment? You don't have to miss it anymore, and you don't have to live in regret over the past.

We all miss some of our moments. Jesus is the only one who's never missed His moment. However, God is faithful, and will always give us more moments. The important thing is that we repent and press forward. The apostle Paul said:

> Not that I have already attained, or am already perfected; but I press on, that I may lay hold of that for which Christ Jesus has also laid hold of

me... one thing I do, forgetting those things which are behind and reaching forward to those things which are ahead, I press toward the goal for the prize of the upward call of God in Christ Jesus.[4]

Kris Vallotton said, "Living in regret will be the greatest thing you end up regretting." Flush the past and move on. When you make a mistake, ask for forgiveness of anyone with whom you've made a mess, and take steps forward. Instead of wallowing in regret, use the pain of missing it to propel you into the next opportunity. The enemy would love nothing more than to rob your future moments with shame to shut you down. Shake it off, and look for the next moment with great hope and anticipation. The Lord who lives outside of time has already crafted more opportunities for you in the future.

In overcoming regret, you must remember that God is a really good Father whose thoughts towards you are perfect. He believes in you more than you believe in yourself, and is not mad at you for missing it.

When my son, Joel, was three years old, I used to take him in the backyard to teach him how to play baseball. I threw many slow pitches at him to try and get him to take a swing and learn what it's like to connect the bat with the ball. Never once did I scold him or get mad at him for missing the ball. It was just the opposite. I celebrated every time he got a little bit closer, until he connected with the ball.

This is how God views us, and how we should view ourselves. This is the perspective we must live from to hit the ball in our next moment. Pick up your bat and get ready, because more pitches are coming today.

---

[4] Philippians 3:12-14

[LET YOUR LIFE SPEAK AND DARKNESS WILL FLEE]

Over 2,700 years ago, God spoke through a prophet named Isaiah:

"Arise, shine; for your light has come!

And the glory of the Lord is risen upon you.

For behold, the darkness shall cover the earth,

and deep darkness the people;

But the Lord will arise over you,

and His glory will be seen upon you."[5]

Jesus is the light that has come, and He declared to us, "*You* are the light of the world."[6] When we believe this proclamation, it empowers us to carry the kingdom of God to dark and uncomfortable places. Just like a lightbulb, we were created to shine and dispel darkness by the flip of a switch.

Darkness has an uncomfortable voice, but it only has power when listened to. We, on the other hand, have a blazing light waiting to be released from the inside of us, and it is the story of how God has touched our lives! Light makes sight possible. When people in darkness hear your story and see your life SPEAK, it will expose the reality in which they're living and give them the opportunity to change.

When standing in front of darkness, it can become uncomfortable to pray for people who are in pain, or to be with people whose lives SPEAK a message that is opposite of what we are carrying. But we cannot retreat to our comfortable forts. The safest place to be is under the shadow of His

---

[5] Isaiah 60:1-5

[6] Matthew 5:14

wing, even if it is in the middle of a battle. Just like Esther, who had to press through uncomfortable feelings and face fear, we must realize that the circumstances are never going to look perfect around us for people to hear our lives SPEAK. We have to ignore the same intimidating spirit that told her to live comfortably quiet, and embrace the call to radically follow Jesus. People on your basketball team, in your class-room, and among your friends are waiting to hear what your life will SPEAK.

When we know that we are alive to please God and not man, the fear of rejection will lose its power, and we will be bold with our light. Rejection is fear with another face on. It attempts to scare us by telling us we're alone or not enough in order to get us to dim our light. If we have already lost our-selves for Jesus' sake, we will be moved by His opinion, not theirs, and we will have power to switch the light on in any atmosphere. I've never seen light be terrified of darkness in a room. It just shines. The light inside of us is stronger than the darkness around us! While many are trying to fit in, we have been called to stand out!

As a new believer, I read these words in the book of Isa-iah: "'Whom shall I send, And who will go for Us?' Then I said, 'Here *am* I! Send me.'"[7] These verses jumped off the page as I read them. Something went off like a lightbulb in my spirit, and this is what my life still SPEAKS today. I re-member shouting in my living room, "Yes, God! Send me. I'll go anywhere!" My heart had been liberated by love, and I wanted the world around me to experience the same love.

Why are we running from the darkness when we have power to quench it? He puts us in front of impossible situa-tions because He, the One who works miracles, is waiting to be released through us. The apostle John said, "The reason

---

[7] Isaiah 6:8

the Son of God appeared was to destroy the devil's work," and "as He is, so are we in this world."[8] We're here to destroy darkness, just as Jesus did!

It's time to run at rejection, run at fear, run at the impossible, and lift up your voice and SPEAK. It is time for your encounters and beliefs in a good God to be heard, experienced, and seen.

If your life once spoke fear, it can now *SPEAK* courage.

If it once spoke shame, it can now *SPEAK* freedom.

If it once spoke doubt, it can now *SPEAK* faith.

If it once spoke rejection, it can now *SPEAK* acceptance.

If it once spoke sinner, it can now *SPEAK* saint.

You are standing in the middle of your moment. Now is the time! Will you let your life *SPEAK*?

---

[8] 1 John 3:8, 1 John 4:17

EPILOGUE

HOW TO BECOME BORN AGAIN

Do you want your life to SPEAK?

Are you feeling stirred by what I talked about in this book?

If so, there's something I need to make sure you know. Your life can only really SPEAK truth and life if you have yourself been introduced to the Truth and the Life. If you don't know what I'm talking about, I would strongly urge you to read these last few pages.

2 CORINTHIANS 5:17

Therefore, if anyone is in Christ, he is a new creation; old things have passed away; behold, all things have become new.

Several years ago, when I was a young teenager, I wrecked my bike in a painful accident. The collision left me with scrapes and scratches all over my legs. As a junior-high boy who had less-than-perfect hygiene, my wounds became infected. As a result, I was exposed to germs that caused me to have a staph infection. Days later, I found myself writhing with excruciating itchiness. No matter how much I scratched, showered, or bandaged myself, relief was nowhere to be found. It was pure torture! The only way to fight this was with the help of an antidote that worked from the inside out. Afterall, it wasn't the visible scrapes and bruises that were tormenting me, it was the infection inside of me. After being properly treated with the correct medication, the staph infection left and the relief was incredible! I felt like I had my life back.

We see and feel the pain in the world. Bullying, racism, war, slavery. While these things are painful and wrong, they are merely the symptoms of an "infection" called sin. A lot of us try to deal with sin by scratching, showering, or bandaging ourselves. Maybe you've tried finding relief from the symptoms. Are you trapped in a lifestyle of living to please other people, even if it means gossiping? Maybe you've turned to porn, premarital sex or others forms of sexual immorality. Maybe you're hanging out with friends you know you shouldn't be or experimenting with drugs and alcohol. The more you try to mask the pain, the worse you feel afterwards. The truth is, there is only ONE healing solution. There's only one person who can truly heal you from the inside out. That person is Jesus Christ. By putting your faith and trust in Him, you're breaking up with sin like it's a bad girlfriend!

ROMAN 6:23

For the wages of sin is death, but the gift of God is eternal life in Christ Jesus our Lord.

The love of God changes everything, and He demonstrates that love through Jesus. The Bible illustrates over and over again how broken people were transformed by an encounter with Jesus. A corrupt tax collector, a prostitute, fishermen, religious leaders, and people oppressed by demons - were all completely changed when they met the love of God through Christ.

It's no different now than it was in the Bible - Jesus wants to meet with you right where you're at and love you in the middle of your mess!

He proved His love by going all the way to the cross to give his sinless life as a ransom for all of humanity. He became the mediator between fallen man and a Holy God. He paid the price for the whole world with His own blood. He took the death we deserved to give us the life He deserved - life everlasting.

His death, burial and resurrection from the grave defeated the devil and all powers of darkness, triumphing over them by the cross. This empowers us to rule in this life as Sons and Daughters of God!

He turns sinners into saints, and gives them a new identity from the inside out. Upon surrendering to Christ He washes us from our past. He no longer sees us through the lenses of our failure, but the lenses of His righteousness!

He will give you a new life and a fresh start, which He calls becoming *born again.*

JOHN 3:3

Most assuredly, I say to you, unless one is born again,
he cannot see the kingdom of God.

Turn to God with all of your heart by **repenting** and **believing** in Jesus.

Repenting means to change the way you think - to do a 180 degree turn from trusting yourself towards trusting Jesus. When we turn to the Lord with our whole heart in surrender, God meets us there with matchless grace and incredible mercy.

Believing in Jesus means trusting what He did on the cross is our source of Salvation. When we truly believe in what He did, we can't help but change. " *I will give you a new heart and put a new spirit in you; I will remove from you your heart of stone and give you a heart of flesh.* Ezekiel 36:26"

Respond to His love and free gift of life today so that your life will SPEAK of redemption and hope for all of eternity! You can pray something like this:

Lord Jesus I come to you just as I am, a sinner. Forgive me, I repent and turn away from trusting my own way and I look to you. I believe you are the Son of God who died in my place and rose from the grave. Thank you for showing me your unconditional love. I confess you to be my personal Lord and Savior. From this day forward, I am yours and you are mine. Come live your life through me. Thank you for loving, saving, and forgiving me. In Jesus name!

Welcome to the family of God. The Bible says you have been born again and you are now a child of God. Receive the Holy Spirit! He will fill you just like He filled the disciples in the Book of Acts. He will be with you always and has promised in his Word, *Never will I leave you and never will I forsake you.* Hebrews 13:5